Prudential Surveillance, Artificial Intelligence and Financial Risk

An Overview of Enhancing Resilience to Financial Crises

Mohamed Miras Marzouki

Prudential Surveillance, Artificial Intelligence and Financial Risk

An Overview of Enhancing Resilience to Financial Crises

ELIVA PRESS

ISBN: 978-99993-3-795-3

Cover Design: Eliva Press
Cover Image: www.ingimage.com
Email: info@elivapress.com
Website: www.elivapress.com

This Eliva Press imprint is published by the registered company Eliva Press Global Ltd. part of Eliva Press S.R.L. Publishing Group

The registered company address is: Pope Hennessy Street Level 2, Hennessy Tower Port Louis, Mauritius
Eliva Press S.R.L. Publishing Group legal address is: Bd. Cuza-Voda 1/4 of. 21, Chisinau, Moldova, Europe

Prudential Surveillance, Artificial Intelligence and Financial Risk

An Overview of Enhancing Resilience to Financial Crises

Part I

PAVING THE WAY FOR ENHANCING STOCK MARKET PRUDENTIAL INTERVENTION THROUGH ARTIFICIAL INTELLIGENCE AND NEURAL NETWORKS

Keywords: Financial stability, Stock market volatility, Distortions, Artificial intelligence, Neural networks, Prudential instruments, Simulation, Economic policy

Abstract

The issue of financial stability and resilience is of commensurate importance for enhancing economic performance and stepping aside the onslaught of financial meltdowns and crises.

There is a consensus that stock market volatility is bound to systemic roots that are afferent to the financial stock market sector trading and are not specific to corporations' performance even though stock market excess volatility can find its roots in corporations' performance which is idiosyncratic and depending on the business cycle phase and the level of advancement of corporations.

The determinants of stock market volatility available in the literature are stock market sector specificities which are auto-correlation of volatility, financial development investor sentiment and Stock market index performance.

This raises a debate on the feasibility of setting a prudential framework for the stock market in concordance with the Basel framework because in analogy with the Basel framework set to curb financial instability coming from the banking sector this prudential framework would curb instability coming from the stock market sector.

Yet one major contingency relates to the fact that prudential authorities are not taking part of transactions that are about trading partners on the stock market and this raises an issue about the feasibility of deploying prudential intervention.

Artificial intelligence can be a major intervenient henceforth and through trading algorithms, deep learning and generative Artificial Intelligence we can impose restrictions shaped accordingly to prudential requirement of targeting the root sources of instability and by the help of deep learning make them adapt to changing conjecture and patterns that evolve over time without recourse to further programming.

This being said, major recommendations can be proposed to the policy maker in terms of enhancing resilience of the financial system from financial instability that might involve both macro-finance and artificial intelligence through imposing restrictions analogous to the Basel framework but whose processing would be enhanced by AI.

1. INTRODUCTION

It is well known that in the context of the Basel frameworks from II to IV prudential instruments are key components engineered to mitigate financial instability in the banking sector.

The Tunisian stock market is still an emerging market presenting opportunities of growth and bearing hindrances of increased risk.

With higher growth comes along according to ARDL surveys on stock market volatility conducted for the Case of Tunisia volatility is found to be positively and significantly correlated with the stock market index which signals forthcoming increased volatility although currently relatively low. And with increased volatility comes along increased financial vulnerability and instability signaling a likely onslaught of financial meltdowns.

Besides the banking sector which is a leading sector in the stock market because of competition displays contrasting performances. Contrasting performances in their turn herald increased volatility.

The competition environment has over the long run an amplification effect on volatility as it motivates contrasting performances inside sectors. As in Tunisia there is much competition inside industries therefore there is a risk of forthcoming onslaught of increased volatility which should be alarming for authorities and justifies the setting of a stock market prudential surveillance toolkit enhanced by artificial intelligence because of unpredictability of the patterns of volatility and the difficulty to proceeding to curbing their pattern on a timely basis.

The apparatus of surveillance is intended to mitigate Market risk pertaining to systemic exposure to excessive volatility and the repercussions of interventions in terms of the market climate reaction to introduced distortions which are the fines resulting from non adherence to restrictions and that are assumed to dissuade investors from anomalous behavior if imposed accurately. Besides concern should be geared toward the exacerbation of anxiety about incurring losses pertaining to regulation that might have unexpected effects due to the complexity and irrationality of investors. As a matter of fact Targeted AI algorithms should code Deep learning about the fundamentals of investor irrationality and smooth forecasts with real figures afferent to this side of factors of influence.

In this respect, the role played by authorities consists in enacting AI based surveillance amending fining processes in compliance with AI forecasts and expectations.

This assumes involving two key concepts which are numerical twins and unconditional simulation simultaneously.

Numerical twins are assumed to generate an upgradable benchmark simulation of the tolerable pattern of volatility gauged by the evolution of volatility within the range of the mainstream caps and ceilings of prudential instruments.

Unconditional simulation is assumed to deal with the repercussions of likely irrational behavior of traders that might emit an unpredictable reaction function to the forecasted effect of the imposed restrictions on volatility of trading and hence generate a self correcting mechanism converging toward the benchmark simulation of numerical twins.

There is scanty scholarly evidence of researchers undertaken for the sake of attempting to curb stock market volatility.

The only reference found in compliance with this subject matter is a paper written by Franklin R Edwards (1988). In his paper, he discusses three clues to curb stock market volatility. But these clues are comparable to "rules of thumb".

They are radical and not in compliance with the requirement of accommodating the healthy stock market climate without reference to their undesirable repercussions of failing to react to how the market responds to these clues and how costly it might reveal in terms of stock market effectiveness and the investment climate not to speak about the interruption or ban of trading (Clue 1) that might reveal catastrophic besides over regulating futures (Clue 2) and reinvigorating derivatives in (Clue 3) which might result in a bubble to burst and hence further exacerbation of the initial hindrance.

In banking sector regulation the regulating item is a part of the issue as the banking sector or the prudential authority in the central bank is the lender of last resort.

But for the stock market sector it is different as trading occurs among investors which are not part of the regulation authority. Besides trading occurs at a fast pace with a huge frequency bypassing thereby human capabilities in proceeding to case by case computations.

This indeed requires coding prudential restrictions by incorporating them in DL algorithms for the sake of annihilating the hindrance of interrupting the natural pace and frequency of transactions which requires also so many computations that humans and administrations such as prudential authorities cannot afford.

We raise a debate and enunciate recommendations afferent to how far does prudential intervention and surveillance of the stock exchange fluctuations can stand for a role played by the government to ensure stock market stability and favor circumvention of excessive market risk and How far do the specificities of AI and Neural network pave the way for deploying accurately prudential intervention and improve effectiveness of forecasting and anomalies for the sake of curbing excess volatility and annihilating hindrances to macro-financial and macro-economic performance distresses.

It is obvious that instability in the financial system does not result exclusively from the instability coming from the banking sector but also from instability coming from the stock market sector that can be expressed in terms of excess volatility and the risk of outburst of stock market crashes.

That is the reason why the policy maker should be specifically concerned about curbing excess volatility in the stock market. This can be achieved as will be thoroughly discussed only via Artificial intelligence based stock market prudential intervention.

2-THE CONTEXT OF THE RESEARCH:

Financial stability is consented in the literature on Macro-finance to be of commensurate importance for issues in economic performance. It is found out in the literature that financial instability or financial vulnerability hampers economic performance.

This called the urge of policy makers to struggle to fight financial instability in various financial sectors to ascertain improved resilience to instability and enhance economic performance.

In the stock market instability emanates essentially from excess volatility of stock market indexes.

Stock market volatility is measured as the difference between the stock market index and the principal component of the stock market which in turn is extrapolated from investor sentiment or investor risk appetite as in the literature see (chart 1) it is mentioned that investor risk appetite s the inverse of the principal component of stock market index so that:

Chart 1: The principal component of the stock market index and the volatility component

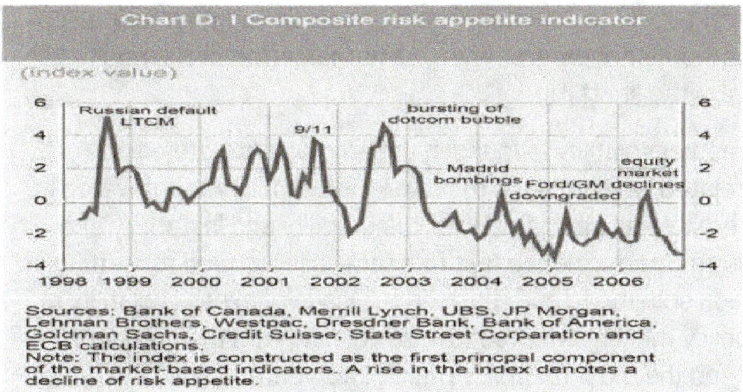

Stock market volatility= Stock market index-principal component of stock market

= Stock market index-(1/investor risk appetite)

The problem is that this being said the modus operandi of a so called prudential toolkit shaped for the stock market sector might be troublesome in face of the changing patterns of sentiment the irrationality of traders and the vast amount of trading and transactions which added to the fact that an eventual prudential authority is not a part to trading like for the Basel framework where the banking credit production is the prudential authority of last resort meaning that the central bank can affect directly the credit production activity through ceilings and caps so that instability is circumvented through restrictions.

This problematic issue can be dealt with, with the help of artificial intelligence which is a key intervenient as far as our subject matter is concerned.

As long as the principal component of the stock market index is the inverse of investor risk appetite it is obvious that the volatility item that represents the scope of this research is bound to investor sentiment.

Empirical evidence in the literature of reference shows that Interest rates do not affect stock market volatility or in other words corporations' performance which is implicitly imbedded in interest rates evolution does not affect stock market volatility.

The market sentiment is found in the empirical literature to react very fast to exogenous shocks in terms of financial development which actually in the process of happening with ongoing introduction of fin-tech and the advancement of digitalization in the banking sector.

Hence in face of this fast reaction of market sentiment and its abrupt repercussions in terms of excess volatility there should be room for neural networks to react without prior programming as human effort is claimed to be slow and ineffectual in the short run.

Besides the stock market volatility is found in the empirical literature to be positively auto-correlated which means that a pike in volatility is aggravated in later lags and exacerbates all along financial vulnerability and instability and might hamper economic performance fast fact that calls the urge for setting an adequate intervention scheme to curb this serious issue of excess volatility in the framework of policy making oriented towards coping with the stakes of financial instability and the must for policy maker intervention.

This leads to ascertain that the effort of curbing excess volatility should not be done at the corporations' level but at the stock market sector level whose volatility reveals significantly affected by its own lag the financial development and investor sentiment

Instead in the stock market not only are trading random but also the behavior of one trader is contingent to irrationality and to sentiment matters.

This motivates the necessity of recourse to Artificial intelligence at a first stage to contain pervasiveness of trading and in a second stage to Neural Networks and Deep learning in order to adapt and upgrade dynamic issues such as unpredicted reaction functions of traders to initial distortions which are fines dissuading from anomalous trading behavior that results in excess volatility that should also be curbed along the volatility issue.

There exists a tradeoff that policy makers must admit and tolerate between FDP finance distorting policies and financial instability.

This can be partially circumvented through AI based simulation that looks for the best timing and magnitude of the distortion dissuading from excess volatility by recourse to deep learning algorithms.

3-THE ANALYSIS AND THE RECOURSE TO ARTIFICIAL INTELLIGENCE

The human based methods of assessments of stock volatility and predicting returns are in many instances ineffectual and portray several shortcomings compared to more sophisticated techniques implied by the recourse to AI.

Zhang (2020) stated that: "although technical analysis and moving averages have been used by investors for years, their vulnerabilities to lagging indicators and market instability validate the use of more efficient and reliable stock prediction methods". And here he refers to AI.

Following the randomness of patterns and investor sentiment whose essentials are not easily depict able and that are usually based on irrationality deep learning and neural networks constitute a key clues to unveil the requirement of a self-sustaining depiction of patterns and early warning to the onslaught of hindrances to stock market financial instability issues. These require timely intervention through restriction based on key sensitivities and ratios that are mainly inscribed in algorithms but whose deploying in time and magnitude require further AI features whose task is the choice of the adequate prudential instrument via neural networks and the timing of intervention with reference to deep learning and trial and error that helps gather patterns and rules.

Cilingtroglu (2023) stated that, "The AI algorithm requires a target variable and model performances on the testing data set would be evaluated through metrics like the Mean Square Error and the average prediction error".

The target variable in the context of our research would be the stock market prudential instrument and the constraints in decision making would be the ceiling or the capping of sensitivities and ratios so as to ensure an impact effect consistent with the requirement of diminishing the instability or the excess volatility of stock market shares which are two notions that go in parallel.

The essential point in recourse to neural networks and deep learning henceforth is as stated by Cilingiroglu (2023) is that: "while learning curves emphasize model performance and precision they also give insights into model bias through the bias variance tradeoff. The point is to balance bias and variance by reducing over fitting and under fitting of expectations by developing models that continuously modify their own nodes. The models apply the multiplicative Weights Method which is an algorithmic technique that provides initial weights to each model then adjust the weights according to their performance in accuracy of prediction".

The analyses of patterns of stock indexes is assumed to provide signals to the generative AI and enact computations at a fast and frequent pace not plausible for human capabilities.

The objective is to learn from the irrationality of evolution of patterns in vicious trends that threaten stability and undesirable evolution of sentiment to warning prematurely from risk of speculative attacks exacerbation of financial instability inscribed in excess volatility of stock indexes that should be regulated through restrictions and fining of key participants in order to curb further excess volatility.

The key rules are the macro prudential, micro prudential and unconventional instruments.

The generative AI is assumed to depict the right timing of intervention and the right choice of prudential instrument to be deployed as well as to enhance neural networks to curb variants in forecasting without recourse to further programming.

Several platforms are readily available for this task among which AI trading. It is currently consented that AI trading involves leveraging artificial intelligence predictive analytical and machine learning to provide past analyses of stock data.

The recourse to Artificial intelligence might rely on detectors of volatility such as VIX tantrum. One example is exhibited in the chart below.

Chart 2: VIX tantrum exhibition: An indicator of volatility in Stock markets

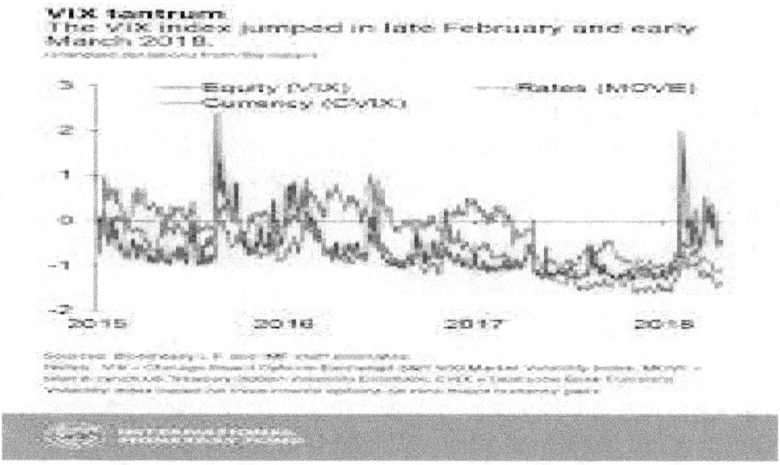

The VIX tantrum is an indicator of sudden pikes in volatility it reflects anxiety or investor low risk appetite in stock market which is a crucial determinant of excess volatility.

The signaling of excess volatility should be coded to act in early warning fashion by detecting prematurely future expected excess volatility and trace back through simulation the badly rated trading that might exacerbated in order to ban their trading smoothly in order to avoid further exacerbation with lagged effects.

The suggested appliances of algorithms should encompass the VIX tantrum indicator in its algorithms and coding in addition to the proposed four types of prudential instruments that are displayed further in the research as thresholds of detection of anomalies and then the recourse to Neural networks void of prior programming fine tunes these indicators to proceed to early warning and intervention based on Deep learning and simulation of likely effects of intervention and restrictions on expected evolution of volatility.

AI enhances decision making in prudential mattes through sentiment analysis which is already available and should be exploited purportedly to grasp sentiment patterns that compromise and exacerbate the financial vulnerability.

Machine learning can refer to key clues or constraints that can be coded and referred to as rules and thereafter applied sequentially in order to filter proceed to early warning and eventually correct any vicious pattern.

Artificial intelligence helps detect vicious patterns apply rules frequently proceed to early warning and facilitation intervention for the sake of mitigating financial instability coming from the stock market sector and by a way of consequence proceeding to stock market prudential surveillance backed by artificial intelligence.

This can be achieved through engineering of macro prudential and micro prudential instruments designed especially to stock market prudential surveillance and would be complementary to the Basel framework for banking sector prudential framework but that would require recourse to AI as it is seemingly unfeasible directly as long as authorities are not a trading part like for credit allocation.

AI applications should incorporate in their design and algorithms key features ensuring improved resilience from vicious patterns that might harm financial stability and proceed to regulation practically like for the Basel framework by fining non respect of prudential restrictions in order to dissuade traders from considering exclusively the search for yield and the manifestation of their sentiment driven choice.

Various algorithms should be shaped for macro prudential and micro prudential instruments having the scope of helping curb vicious patterns that exacerbate exposure to financial instability while ensuring the flexibility of trading and free choice simultaneously.

This task would be unfeasible through human effort and require recourse to Artificial Intelligence and Deep Learning that ascertains upgrading without recourse to additional programming.

4. THE METHODOLOGICAL APPROACH OF INCORPORATING ARTIFICIAL INTELLIGENCE IN PRUDENTIAL SURVEILLANCE

Artificial intelligence is assumed in analogy with the traditional use of forecasting future trends and prices of stock markets to be used to predict future volatility by including prudential surveillance tools as captors to disentangle abusive trading to the compliance with prudential requirements of safeguarding tolerable volatility and neural networks depict anomalous patterns based on learning from analyses from previous episodes of high volatility in concordance with its fundamental description of the climate of its ignition and proceed to fining of abusively distant figures from caps and ceilings so that the pattern of volatility is curbed correspondingly to financial instability mitigation requirements.

The macro-prudential and micro-prudential instruments should be incorporated into the coding of Artificial Intelligence as prior binding constraints. Then machine learning can adapt timing of reaction so as not to risk to react lately after episodes of high volatility has ignites and avoid to intervene precautious in order to limit the frictions and distortions entailed prudential restrictions that by abusively distorting the natural flow of trading can reveal harmful for the trading climate.

Further insights can be grasped through assessing the impact of fining and restrictions on the investment climate so that machine learning can fine-tune restrictions and fining not to introduce a bias in investor climate in compliance with the requirement of favoring a healthy trading climate which is important for financial and economic performance.

Prudential instruments are computed instantaneously on a continuous bases then caps and ceilings are fixed as thresholds.

And captors signal bypassing and fine exuberant bypassing for traders so that vicious practices that result in excessive volatility are curbed and mitigation of financial instability is improved.

The process of anomalous trading fining intended to curb malicious patterns of excess volatility should not be implemented right away.

But those malicious patterns should be subject to rating like in credit rating and fines imposed corresponding to the process of setting risk premiums where risk stands for the likelihood in resulting in excess volatility.

For this sake deep learning is implemented to afford learning from past performance of trading clusters with respect to the extent of their effect on stimulating excess volatility.

The final objective is to curb excess volatility and mitigate financial instability while at the same time to safeguard a healthy investment climate as trading might be biased through fining which might be compromising for efficiency of the stock market by introducing distortions that affect efficiency and effectiveness that would have occurred had trading been void from distortions.

For this sake deep learning helps curb excess volatility while learning and updating restrictions in accordance to their effect on investment and trading climate.

Besides, deep learning can proceed to rating of anomalies to impose fines once ratings degradation and readjust the tendency with the help of simulation when trading climate is compromised through deep learning.

Macro prudential intervention through predictive AI and simulation with thresholds on ratios of caps and ceilings can be subjected to upgrading depending on how the software learns from previous effectiveness measurement of the impact of prudential intervention on excess volatility. Micro-prudential intervention through Deep learning and Neural networks proceedings to rating analogous to credit rating requires learning from previous excess volatility episodes and scoring of corporations and traders but programming is not sufficient. Hence the coding learning from its previous performance as trading at the micro level is so frequent and voluminous that programming cannot be adjusted and hence the software has to learn from previous performance continuously.

5. A SCHEMATICAL REPRESENTATION OF THE PROCESS OF INVOLVMENT OF ARTIFICIAL INTELLIGENCE AND SIMULATION WITH DEEP LEARNING AND OVERLAPPING UPGRADING:

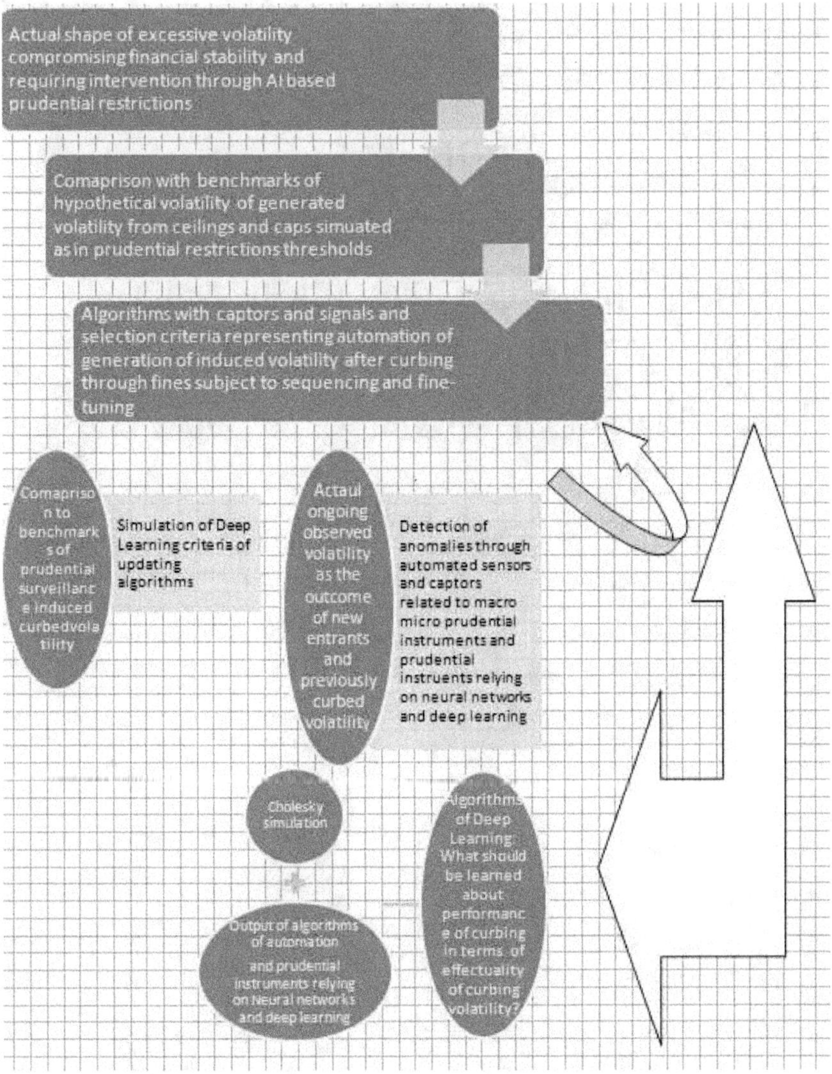

Part II

STOCK MARKET PRUDENTIAL SURVEILLANCE TOOLKIT AND CONCEPTUAL FRAMEWORK FOR INTEGRATION OF FINANCIAL SECTORS

Keywords

Overreaction, UnderReaction, Volatility, Prudential Regulation, Market Risk, Hedging, Efficiency,

Investor Sentiment, Financial Stability, Macroprudential, Microprudential, Collision, Balanced Scorecard, Borrowers' creditworthiness, Non performing Loans

Abstract

This part is an attempt to engineer a prudential toolkit for the stock market analogous to the Basel toolkit in its second third and fourth versions.

It raises the concern about the requirement of mitigating market risk coming from excess volatility of share prices that compromises financial stability and argues that mitigating credit market risk like in the Basel prudential surveillance systembis insufficient to provide accurate resilience from the onslaught of financial meltdowns.

A clear specification of stock market efficiency paves the way for an accurate understanding of the key features pertaining to the Stockbmarket sectorcdefining financial stability and drawing à wedge to shaping à framework for setting à prudential toolkit through adopting an analogy methodology with the Basel framework.

The issue of integration of financial sectors is conveyed a prominant role in all its aspects of collision between instruments, the role played by the balanced scorecard and the induction of instability from the credit sector features of credit information assymetries borrowers Creditworthiness and non performing loans through the financial accelerator effect to the excess volatility of share prices and elucidates thereby the way financial sectors are integrated.

The issue of hedging raises a concern about the role it plays in prudentiality and the potential threat it might represent for credit risk financial stability.

Finally a general appraisal on stability and efficiency is framed in perspective forvtrading in the primary and secondary markets.

1. Introduction

The Stock market stability matters because a stock market's vulnerability in promptly responding to outside stimuli provides accurate and up to date information about the entire financial market and economy. These in turn affect commensurately global investor sentiment and their willingness to fuel capital inflows inside the country which constitute a leakage for the financial system overall to ensure availability of liquidity and credit for the various financial sectors; the credit sector, the insurance sector, the stock market sector.

Stock market prudential surveillance and intervention schemes reveal to be a must as prudential surveillance for the credit sector as being displayed in the Basel frameworks does not mitigate financial instability coming from the Stock market sector.

It is intended to target mitigating Market risk pertaining to systemic exposure to excessive volatility and the repercussions of over-reaction and under reaction to earnings that exacerbate market excessive volatility and the resulting financial instability.

In this respect, the role played by authorities consists in mitigating stock market instability and avoiding the contingency of occurrence of market crashes.

Stock market stability includes covariance between macroeconomic fundamentals relative to business cycle fluctuations and returns on equity as well as investor sentiment and risk appetite.

How far does prudential intervention and surveillance of the stock exchange fluctuations can stand for a role played by the government to ensure stock market stability and favor circumvention of excessive market risk?

What instruments grasp most the basics of threats accompanying uncertainty, excessive fluctuations of equity prices, contagion and systemic market risk?

We attempt also to analyse how does the integration financial financial sectors occur ?

How does financial instability in the credit market compromise financial instability in the Stock market ?

How is collision and the Balanced scorecard involved in the integration process across fnancial sectors ? and finally we try to explore what is the role played by hedging in mitigating financial instability.

2. A PRIMER TO STOCK MARKET STABILITY AND EFFICIENCY

As long as the stock market is of commensurate importance for economic performance considerations, there is a longstanding interdependence between macroeconomic aggregates and stock market financial items emphasizing the channels through which a shock in the stock market propagates to the economy and affects economic performance as stated in Sajjad, Noreen, & Zaman (2013) that reiterated the main findings of a research undertaken by Pilinkus (2010) indicating while emphasizing on the dependence of stock market on the macroeconomic indicators by running co-integration tests such as Johansen and Vector autocorrection that: "Johansen co-integration tests signified that the stock market and the macroeconomic factors have a long term relationship and the stock market is somewhat dependent on the macroeconomic variables of the economy".

According to Shreya & Sangeetha (2019): "Irrespective of the country, the macroeconomic variables have a significant effect not only on the capital market but also on the businesses and the macroeconomic factors affect the investment risk in any country."

According to Son et al. (2009): "A stable stock market is essential to the entire financial system and economy stressing the significance of monitoring the stability of the stock market."

Therefore the requirement for shaping a prudential framework stems from the need of ensuring stability and preserving it with intervention and supervision in order to ascertain an adequate pattern of economic growth.

Indeed, according to the super-multiplier theory firstly posited by P A Samuelson and J R Hicks which is an effect that results from the interaction between the financial accelerator and the Keynesian multiplier or a combined leverage effect: "the interaction of the multiplier and accelerator is capable under certain circumstances of generating continuous cyclical fluctuations. The effects of financial imbalances translate into greater effects on the macroeconomic situation. This is where acceleration principle stems from".

To give a brief reminder of the supermultiplier theory which is of prominant relevance for the subject matter, J R Hicks (1950) has interacted both the multiplier effect of Keynes and the accelerator effct of Aftalian with a view of measuring the total effect of induced investment on income.

The combined effect of multiplier that works converse to crowding out and accelerator is the so-calledleverage effect or the supermultiplier effect.

P A Samuelson (1939) in his article about the interaction between the multiplier and the principal of acceleration and J R Hicks later in (1950) have made successful attempts to integrate the two concepts of financial acceleration and Keynesian multiplier which works converse to our crowding out effect matter and thus introduced remarkable improvements in the theory of economic growth.

They stated it is important to analyse the compbined effects or leverage effect or supermultiplier effect oon national income propagation.

The combination of autonomous and induced investment is a better expression of this supermultiplier as stated by Hansen.

The relevance of the supermultiplier to prudential matters stems from the fact that it draws a wedge between financial instability as portrayed by excess volatility of stock prices and macroeconomic performance that affects companies net worth and reverses back to the matter of prudentiality through the leverage effect and the tradeoff of equity financing and external borrowing.

As far as this arbitrage between various sources of financing for corporations is concerned the banking sector liquidity and credit risk features are quite intricating with respect to the setting of the cost of borrowing for corporations.

Thus all these aspects of financial accelerator supermultiplier and market risk are commingled to feed back into excess stock prices volatility and fuel financial instability and the requirement of limiting it through prudential intervention either in the credit sector or the Stock market sector .

The issue of efficiency is of commensurate importance in describing the root cause of financial instability.

Some authors advocate that inefficiency justifies financial instability and that it is the rationale for requiring a prudential framework whose scope is to ascertain mitigated market risk in order to attenuate financial instability.

2.1. MARKET RISK, VOLATILITY AND COVARIANCE BETWEEN STOCK RETURNS

Adrian & Rosenberg (2008) explore the cross-sectional pricing of volatility risk by decomposing equity market volatility into short- and long-run components. Their finding is that: "Prices of risk are negative and significant for both volatility components implies that investors pay for insurance against increases in volatility, even if those increases have little persistence. The short-run component captures market skewness risk, which they interpret as a measure of the tightness of financial constraints. The long-run component relates to business cycle risk. Furthermore, a three-factor pricing model with the market return and the two volatility components compares favorably to benchmark models".

2.2. TRADING CHOICE MAKING BASED ON INVESTOR SENTIMENT AND FIRMS CHARACTERISTICS

We attempt to provide two measures of stock market stability displaying two various purviews having various scopes.

One measure relates to the macroeconomic purview of the definition of stability implications, whereas, the second one displays an efficiency purview.

1) The macroeconomic purview:

The compounded Stock market stability index is the inverse of the propensity of stock volatility computed as the product of two indexes one measuring the amplitude of the core industry where ignition of contagion in stock prices patterns originates from or the source of contagion powered by the extent of contagion or how volatility propagates and the other measuring covariance between stock prices volatility and the business cycle phase including stock market efficiency.

Indeed, as long as partial Pareto optimality means inexistence of idiosyncratic diversification, the pattern of volatility is commensurately covariant with irrational sentiment based speculation whereby as market values are close to book values there is no arbitrage making whenever the market is efficient and henceforth efficiency measures the extent of instability.

It stands that as market values are nearly identical to book values the shape of business cycle matters and their effects on production capacity provides assessment of the volatility of market values of stock prices via the dividend channel of transmission of volatility that transfers fluctuations from production capacity to book and market values assuming that market values are exogenous somehow to traders when markets are efficient and supply of stock is dependent on production capacity.

Stock Market Stability Index = [(Market Value of Core Industry (Market sentiment))*OG*(∑Market to book values)] - 1

As long as absence of arbitrage prospects is beneficial for speculators, irrational investors driven by sentiment guide market risk towards excess volatile profitability expected aspects of stock prices.

Hence, stock market stability goes in reverse direction with overall profitability of trading.

2) The Stock market efficiency purview:

The stock market stability index should be measured in terms of the dispersion of the impact effect of incremental modifications of factors of prominent relevance involving both stability and efficiency criteria.

As a matter of fact, as long as stability and efficiency in its semi-strong form represent a conundrum involving both arbitrage and sentiment due to the clear tradeoff between them and obvious must of affording both of them, it is obvious that fathoming one criterion either stability or efficiency should be conditional on the other in reference to the famous economic concept of opportunity cost.

Our fundamental figure grasping simultaneously most of aspects salient to these both issues and compromising both investor risk appetite and irrational sentiment is the price to earnings ratio.

Indeed, this ratio, although simple, provides accurate information about the nature of the firm whose stakes are traded. As the (price to earnings) ratio varies the qualification of traded stakes vary from most rationally based on arbitrage and historical accounting value analysis to the least rationally based on intuitive sentiment and gambling distinguished by determinants that are tough to grasp.

The price to earnings ratio informs also on the availability of information salient to the firm whose shares are traded but also whether the efficient market hypothesis holds or not. Most important of all it informs on the closeness of the market to the book value which is rudimental for a clear assessment of the willingness of investors to speculate and by a way of consequence assessed in sensitivity or impact effect of incremental variations of price to earnings ratio can provide an early warning scheme whereby we can gauge the extent to which there is salient threat of speculation compromising stability of the stock market.

Thus, by computing the elasticity of market to book value of shares to price to earnings ratio we can provide a tool of commensurate importance for stability assessment which might be called; the dispersion of the opportunity cost between the willingness to speculate based on sentiment and the Pareto improvement affordable through arbitrage based trading in the stock market.

This is the standard deviation of the elasticity of market to book values of shares to price to earnings ratio.

Stability index = Standard deviation {e(MBV/(Price/Earning)

2.3. INVESTOR RISK APPETITE : A GENERAL APPRAISAL

Investor risk appetite as shown in the following chart displaying its average shape world-wide, is following a pattern of alternations between pikes and troughs meaning that it is either pro-cyclical in phase with the business cycle or countercyclical but anyway not a-cyclical.

Therefore there is a strong correlation between business fluctuations in investor risk appetite suggesting a string relationship between market risk and instability and the business cycle fluctuations.

Therefore the consensus that the main trigger of volatility comes from new comes and research and Development industries and firms subjected to restructuration and bankruptcy is subject to criticism because as long as business cycle fluctuations affect considerably investor risk appetite there are skepticism about the role played by the main sources of excessive volatility causing financial instability that are found out in the literature to be unpredictable.

Indeed the main source of financial instability comes from those businesses whose profitability prospects are predictable if not investor confidence would have not been responsive to business fluctuations meaning cyclical. This is indeed not the case.

Chart D. I Composite risk appetite indicator

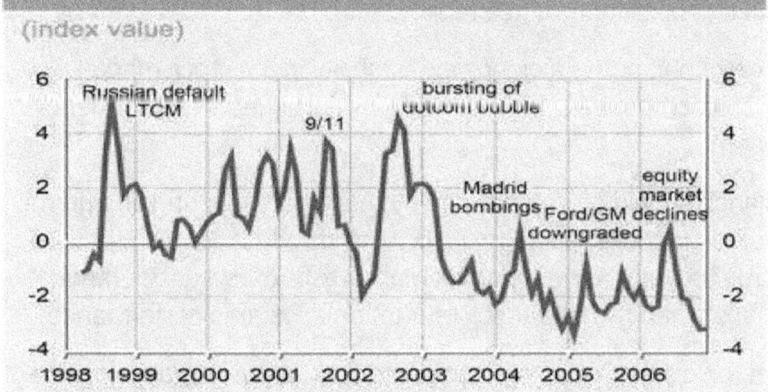

Sources: Bank of Canada, Merrill Lynch, UBS, JP Morgan, Lehman Brothers, Westpac, Dresdner Bank, Bank of America, Goldman Sachs, Credit Suisse, State Street Corparation and ECB calculations.
Note: The index is constructed as the first princpal component of the market-based indicators. A rise in the index denotes a decline of risk appetite.

It is noteworthy to state here that investor risk appetite is inversely proportional to the pikes in the market based principal components.

As a matter of fact as there is a pike in the market based principal component following a conjectural event having an effect of an upswing or downswing in the market index, the investor risk appetite behaves cotrariwise to it.

With respect to the conjecture, investor risk appetite is countercyclical to most prominant conjectural events meaning that as volatility increases the predisposition of investors to bear excessive risk as defining their risk appetite declines contrariwise to the movement in fluctuations in either case a sharp increase or a sharp decline.

This can be interpreted that the commonsense risk appetite of investors has got a preference of periods of tranquility in the fluctuations of market indicators.

Indeed, in terms of forecasting the market behavior it is far better affordable to have a clear foresightedness of the market tendency although not necessarily true in periods of tranquility of market indicators than in periods of excessive volatility where it is far more difficult to give a clear foresifghtedness of how the market would behave and thereafter be likely to bear excesive risk or not depending on the risk appetite of the defined investor.

2.4. STOCK MARKET EFFICIENCY

Efficiency of equilibrium in the stock market is measured in terms of market value premium over book value. This means essentially that stock market efficiency is inversely proportional to its stability.

The hindrance of gathering both efficiency and stability in the stock market raises the debate of incompatibility between prudential aspects and efficiency aspects in equilibrium.

Prudential surveillance should be constrained by the task of favoring an optimal efficient market value of stocks if not the distortions introduced by Prudential instruments become too expensive for stock market efficiency considerations and for the effect of efficiency of the stock market on economic performance.

As a matter of fact the market value of firms is a driver for performance added value and future expansionary capacity that promotes economic growth.

Can stock market efficiency be considered as a prudential instrument or an early warning instrument enabling to provide forward guidance for market risk expectations and future patterns?

Stock market efficiency is closely linked to Pareto optionality a situation where we can't improve a situation of one dealer without deteriorating the situation of one other.

Indeed stock market instability comes from the deterioration of the situation of several factors that propagates to others until there exists a market crash.

Thus in other words stock market efficiency goes in the same direction with stock market instability.

The optimal situation would be a situation where we can improve the position of some speculators without deteriorating that of others.

Market sentiment and irrational decision making about trading based on absence of arbitrage further exacerbates the pattern of fluctuations and volatility with speculation based on rumors and lack of information that triggers limitation and motivates excess volatility.

In the case on non Pareto optimality the fact that the situation of some traders improves without deteriorating that of others slows down the excess volatility reigning over the stock market trading because the latter can be better off without imitating the former. By a way of consequence stock prices fluctuations are average and volatility is not excessive.

Efficiency of equilibrium in the stock market is measured in terms of market value premium over book value. This means essentially that stock market efficiency is inversely proportional to its stability.

The hindrance of gathering both efficiency and stability in the stock market raises the debate of incompatibility between prudential aspects and efficiency aspects in equilibrium.

Indeed as efficiency improves there is more room for Pareto optimality. Which means that we can less improve the situation of several traders without deteriorating that of others? This can be achieved viewed macro economically whenever the market to book value decreases to less than one.

This also stands for a prerequisite of increased instability or deteriorated stability because as efficiency improves and book value is close to market value, volatility of stock market is very sensitive to business cycle fluctuations and irrational investors are more driven by sentiment as long as the difference between market value to book value stands for an rationally based indicator of future earnings prospects. This means that through increased trading of speculators driven by irrational sentiment volatility of stock prices increases and by a way of consequence stock market stability deteriorates.

Stock market efficiency is measured in terms of degree of partial optimality in other words how far several traders can be better off without deteriorating other traders' earnings situation.

The more the Stock market is efficient the fewer traders are better off without deteriorating other traders' earnings.

According to Dimson & Massoud (1998): "The available theory of market efficiency involves defining an efficient market as one in which trading on available information fails to provide an abnormal profit. A market can be deemed to be efficient therefore only if we posit a model for returns. From this point tests of market efficiency become joint tests of market behavior and models of asset pricing. But long term mispricing however could constitute a serious violation of market efficiency. Stocks which have underperformed the most over a three to five year period average the highest market adjusted return of the subsequent period and vice versa.

A return reversal is overreaction to market in which stock prices diverge from fundamental values. There is short run positive correlation among stock returns and long run negative correlation which leads to overreaction and under-reaction".

A theoretical normative explanation of efficiency and inefficiency is given by Joseph (1982) in his theoretical work. Entitled: "The inefficiency of stock market equilibrium" where he provides an analytical proof of the inefficiency of market equilibrium

According to him: "the widespread view that the market equilibrium is efficient is only true fort the special case when there is one commodity because any changes n the allocation of investment on the distribution of ownership shares in the efficient assets will change the distribution in prices. Hence, the nature of risky assets which are marketed changes. Since there are incomplete risks markets, this change in the nature of risky assets which are available has welfare effects which need to be taken into account. There are two sets of restrictions on preferences which will guarantee that the market will be efficient. The distribution of ownership claims has no effect on price distribution only if individuals have identical homotetic indifference curves. But changes in the allocation of investment have no effects only if there is no trade because all individuals are identical or when there is no effective risk because all individuals have the same demand curve with unitary price elasticity. These assumptions are inelastic therefore market equilibrium is inefficient".

Hence, these statements affect the relationship of stock market prices volatility patterns covariance with the business cycle. Indeed, as long as stock market is more efficient, market values of stocks close to book values. This makes trading affect commensurately production capacity as long as stock prices are inversely proportional to dividends that are a trigger of shareholders willingness to inject equity in firms. By a way of consequence, the more stock market is efficient the more the pattern of stock tradings is covariance with the business cycle.

Stated otherwise, as stock market becomes more efficient stock demand higher share prices and by a way of consequence lowers dividends and increases demand for credit.

This is how the credit market is compromised.

But as long as prices rise in the stock market credit risk does the same accordingly.

As credit risk increases so does the willingness of the banking system to bear more risk and NCPS. So from the IS-LM representation output gap becomes lower and business cycles are shorter when demand of stocks is in excess and share prices are rising.

Contrariwise when supply of stocks is higher and share prices are declining business cycle length is higher.

Seen otherwise, increased covariance between business cycle phase and stock prices makes expansionary phases increase production and book value and with increased stock market efficiency market value in parallel which decreases dividends and increases NCPS and thereby shortens the business cycle or decreases output gap.

PROOF:

We refer to the aggregate demand aggregate supply equilibrium and adjustment in the IS-LM Keynesian backed theory for a closed economy to simplify the analysis.

As a matter of fact, for increases in money market rates for a certain level of real interest rate, inflation is assumed to increase, which is interpreted in the IS-LM model as an increase in the price level. The adjustment in the equilibrium between aggregate demand and aggregate supply makes them shift to the right and shows a decrease in output gap for increases in propensity to invest that steepen the aggregate demand curve.

This slope increases with increases in i' which is the propensity to invest.

By totally differentiating the IS and LM curves equations we find that:

$$Y = c\left(y - t(y)\right) + i(r) + g$$

By differentiation: $\mathrm{d}y = c'(1-t)\mathrm{d}y + i'\mathrm{d}r + \mathrm{d}g$

$$M/P = l(r) + k(y)$$

By differentiation: $1/p\,\mathrm{d}M - M/p^2\,\mathrm{d}P = l'\mathrm{d}r + k'\mathrm{d}y$

So that: $\mathrm{d}r = \left(1/(l' * p)\right)\mathrm{d}M - \left(M/\left(l' * p^2\right)\right)\mathrm{d}P - (k'/l')\mathrm{d}y$

Substituting into dy leads to:

$$\mathrm{d}y = c'(1-t)\mathrm{d}y + i'\left(\left(1/(l' * p)\right)\mathrm{d}M - \left(M/\left(l' * p^2\right)\right)\mathrm{d}P - (k'/l')\mathrm{d}y\right) + \mathrm{d}g$$

Therefore, the aggregate demand slope which is equl to $\mathrm{d}y/\mathrm{d}P$

is $\mathrm{d}y/\mathrm{d}P = -\left((i'/l')M\right)/\left(\left(1 - c'(1-t')\right) + i'(k'/l')\right)$

Therefore, when the aggregate demand slope increases, the aggregate demand curve becomes steeper and OG lower or decrease the propensity to invest increases and so does investment.

Contrariwise, during contraction phases production decreases and book value of firms decreases but with increased stock market efficiency market value decreases which augments dividends and decreases NCPS and by a way of consequence augments output gap. This makes business cycles longer.

Therefore, as stock markets are more efficient expansionary phases are shorter and recessionary phases are longer.

In conclusion stock market efficiency is harmful for economic performance.

As long as stock market efficiency is opposed to stock market stability, it follows that stock market stability is beneficial for economic performance.

Therefore stock market stability has to be promoted. This can be purportedly achieved through prudential surveillance whose instruments are shaped to motivate increased stock market stability and whose aim is to promote stock market stability.

3. THE STOCK MARKET PRUDENTIAL FRAMEWORK

3.1. RATIONALE FOR SETTING A PRUDENTIAL TOOLKIT

Market inefficiency through overreaction and under-reaction discussed above, is the main root of the onslaught of systemic excessive volatility leading to financial instability and the risk of the onslaught of stock market hindrances to tranquility and eventually meltdowns and stock crashes.

This is the fundamental reason justifying the requirement of setting a prudential framework aiming at engineering surveillance instruments whose purpose is to ascertain complete resilience from financial instability or at least containing it at the maximum in order to avoid dangerous financial meltdowns and the risk of outburst of stock crashes.

So the first reason for setting a prudential toolkit is comprehensive and relates to the inability of Basel II, III and IV agreements which are specific to the credit sector surveillance to be valid for ascertaining stock market prudential surveillance.

And the second reason is analytical and relates to the fact that stock market inefficiency which has been discussed above exacerbates financial instability in a way that dismays resilience from financial meltdowns which requires setting a prudential framework targeting the stock market anomalies specifically.

3.2 PRUDENTIAL INSTRUMENTS ENGINEERING

The structural form of prudential instruments is inspired from both the ratio based structure of Basel II and III framework and the complementary method of sensitivity analyses proposed by Marzouki M in his unpublished Phd dissertation (2022): "A theory of strategic financial foresight and prudential engineering: Case of Tunisia."

The structural form or mathematical formula matters a lot as will be shown as each formula plays a certain role having specific economic and financial implication.

The root market generator of speculation and systemic market risk exposure that is the basic source of market risk fluctuations that are not pertaining to arbitrage and trigger most of market volatility and uncertainty is a certain combination of the key industries in extreme dependency to volatility and contagion.

The issue of randomness of stock prices volatility seldom heralds opportunities of optimal diversification and represents a major cause of market risk and threat to stock market stability and the risk of a collapse.

This issue heralds in unpredictability and high covariance of fundamental items pertaining to the stock market making contagion through excessive volatility and hence likely exacerbation of meltdowns or collapse and other troublesome scenarios of undesirable implications of commensurate importance and relevance to investors' earnings occur.

Macro prudential instruments should take the form of ratios because they are intended to grasp the covariance between the business cycle fluctuations and investor sentiment implications on market volatility which reveals to be dependent on caps and ceilings of proportions including firms' production and dividend policies as major factors drawing a wedge between market valuation and business cycle dependent production demand fluctuations whereas micro prudential instruments should take the form of elasticity because as long as investor sentiment is irrational and implies concern with excess volatility, its irrationally based volatility should be fathomed through impact effects involving causality, interconnectedness and interdependencies.

The difference between methodologies adopted in both frameworks is due to the shape and extent of covariance between interdependent volatilities whereby the stake of volatility plays a prominent role in determining the mathematical formula of the restriction that fits better to unvell the threat involved and that reveals compromising to market stability and build adequate resilience from it in both frameworks.

By a way of consequence, the Macro prudential framework methodological approach is "Up to Bottom" based; and focuses on covariance between business cycle and market prices expectations about production policy that affects the shape of stock market and share prices as being commensurately dependent on production and economic activity performance and fluctuations across the business cycle

Whereas, in the micro prudential framework, the methodological approach is

«Bottom to Up» and focuses on that bothers irrational investors or traders that mainly are not rational arbitrageurs rather they are characterized by irrationally based decision making driven by sentiment for whom determinants and fundamentals are difficult to grasp or model.

As a matter of fact, according to Baker & Wargler (2007): "The top down approach focuses on the measurement of reduced form aggregate sentiment and traces its effects to market returns and individual stocks. Whereas, the new direction in the top down approach build on the two broader and more influential assumptions of behavioral finance namely sentiment and limits to arbitrage to explain which stocks are likely to be most affected by sentiment rather than simply pointing out the level of qtock prices in the aggregate depends on sentiment . In particular, stocks of low capitalization, younger, unprofitable, high volatility, non-dividend paying growth companies or stocks of firms in financial distress are likely to be disproportionately sensitive to brad waves of investor sentiment".

Therefore, restrictions in this framework should focus on binding sensitivity of certain items to others because excess volatility is mainly fathomable through impact effect of the sort that is graspable by the elasticity that is a best mathematical measure of the excesses of financial volatility.

Prudential instruments are aimed at motivating Stock market stability. They are restrictions comparable to the Basel II, III and IV agreements setting prudential toolkit for the Stock market restrictions framework.

They aim at mitigating Stock market volatility and better shaping interdependency between volatile stocks and sentiment impact on key root industries where contagion of excess volatility propagates from. In addition they provide a framework of resilience from speculative attacks that result from mass purchases or sell offs that are badly intended to affect the overall information available for traders.

Shaping a prudential scheme for prudential intervention whose scope is to enhance resilience from these effects is an endeavoring task entitled to engineer instruments taking the form of ratios or elasticity fashioned with respect to the same methodology as in Basel II, III and IV agreements pertaining to Banking sector prudential surveillance.

The issue of volatility and contagion can be adequately assessed exclusively through a mathematical tool that measures impact effects of incremental variations which is the elasticity. Macro prudential intervention might be related to covariance between business cycle and market behavior while Micro prudential intervention is essentially related to the dividend policy and rent of capital issues that exert an effect on expectations of future returns.

The macro-prudential instruments engineering method derives from the empirical findings about the determinants of stock returns as explained by Fama & French (1992) where Daxhammer & Kappler (2016) reiterated that: "According to the CAPM only one single risk factor the market beta is sufficient to determine stock returns. But Fama and French in their empirical work examined the effect of several factors on average stock returns and come out to the conclusion that beta does not seem to help explain the cross section of average stock returns. In contrast, they found significant evidence that the combination of firm size and book to market equity (BE/ME) absorbs the role of the other tested variables which are financial leverage to earnings to price ratio for determining stock returns"

We emphasize the role of these factors in shaping macro-prudential instruments while capping them or ceiling them accordingly to whether their increase affects financial stability negatively or positively respectively.

The more the firm is new comer with unpredictable shape of expected earning or the more the firm is financially distressed the higher is the markup and the more demand it can tolerate once the restriction is imposed.

Macro prudential instruments are methodologically set up to bottom because mainly macro prudential framework is related to the covariance between the business cycle and the stock prices and therefore implies policy and restrictions on items related to firms' management with respect to both the corporate profitability depending on the phase of the business cycle and the corporate dividend policy binding the asset prices whose volatility is in congruence with business cycle implications on production capacity. Instead, micro prudential instruments relate to attenuating volatility implied by irrational investors neither acting like arbitrageurs nor like risk adverse investors.

3.3 MACROPRUDENTIAL INSTRUMENTS

Instrument 1:

- Caps on (Dividends/Cost of borrowing) or so the called "cost of capital ratio".

If (dividends/cost of borrowing) ratio increases then the management team decision making will be sensitive to stakeholders investment sentiments. This in turn will induce a bias in the volatility of the share prices and their covariance with overall share prices that affect stakeholders' decision making about arbitrage related to equity distributed among the various firms. Share prices when assessed by their book value that is set through the expectations and financial accounting of the firm's managers and for a given efficiency of the stock market that mainly affects the market to book value, an increase in the ratio will make volatility and covariance between stocks increase far beyond tolerable by the prudential authority.

Therefore it has to cap it through a restriction to avoid excess volatility to exacerbate financial instability.

Instrument 2:

- Caps on (Equity/Expected return on industry) or the so called "sensitivity of stakeholders to profitability of companies".

This instrument is based on the principal that whenever stakeholders are too responsive to increases in expected returns in an industry they are attracted in, there will be a bias in amplification of volatility of stock prices and excessive cross correlation between firms acting in the same industry generating thereby a hindrance to financial stability.

Therefore, prudential regulation should consider alleviating this hindrance through capping or limiting the ratio of equity of firms to the expected return of the industry they are acting in.

Instrument 3:

- Ceilings on (Tangible assets/Equity) or the so called "volatility induced allocation of equity".

Now from the standpoint of the management teams of corporations, there should be more concern about diminishing subjectively priced assets or those whose value is cross correlated to an issue pertaining to the same industry or the business cycle. Instead, tangible assets are secure assets in the sense they are like a store of value for the book value of the firm and are least subject to fluctuations whenever there is a case of considering the gap between the market value and the book value. As a matter of fact intangible assets are more likely to be assessed by their market values than tangible assets. Eventually there is a hindrance in having market and book values too close drawing a wedge of traceability for speculators that can make sure about the rationale lying behind the discrepancies between book and market values and correct their behavior correspondingly o what should be done to avoid to be driven by sentiment or speculation based decision making more than having a clear idea about what is happening when book and market values are far from each other.

Instrument 4:

- Ceiling on Covariance between External borrowing and internal borrowing or what is called "countercyclical financial accelerator buffers".

This instrument is comparable to the first instrument as it helps diversify the source of volatility and cross correlation between the determinants of internal borrowing that mainly are fundamentally related to correlation to other stock prices whereas external borrowing is dependent on credit market conditions whose volatility is dissipated in the banking sector and retraceable only through the banking decision making through the search for yield channel whenever they hold a vast proportion of assets in the form of shares in other corporations but at least not depending on the credit market conditions where most correlation stems from monetary policy conditions.

The principal is comparable to the countercyclical capital buffers of the Basel Framework for credit market prudential surveillance but it applies to the notion of financial accelerator explained more in depth later in the research in the reference by Fender (2000) in the next chapter.

Instrument 5 : Cross sector exacerbation of Market risk

Ratio (Listed hedged securities/Non performing loans of the corporations issuing those securities)

When the ratio of hedged securities on non performing loans of the corporations issuing those securities increases, the derivatives warant hints more the threat that comes from the fact that mainly the profitability of trading a non hedged security is a signal of the health of the corporation issuing the security.

In other words, the increase in the amount of derivatives in itself might signal an improvement in stcok market stability as hedging works as a prudential surveillance instrument because it shields from the risk of failure and by a way of consequence crush if aggregated.

But at the same time, as more shielding of unsound management of corporations (which is indeed the case if not hedging would have not been adopted as it assumes that the likelihood of failing the trade is commensurate for a certain risk aversion) might signal an increase in default of payments of loans which might exacerbate credit market risk far beyond expected.

Indeed, as more leakage is intrduced to those unsoudly managed corporations that because of purchase of derivatives end up with better securitisation hence better equity and investments in plants and equipement and eventually more external borrowing and more non performing loans at higher borrowing rates compensating the banks from the increase in the risk of default with higher, risk premiums.

Therefore, there should be a capping for this ratio as a prudential instrument for resilience from Stock market risk of instability in that it caps the quantity of derivatives with respect to the available information on the historical data on default of repayment of external debt through bank based borrowing.

Instrument 6 : The supermultiplier ratio

The ratio (Average Net worth of corporations/Dividends volatility) should be ceiled sothat the contagion of excess stock market volatility does not propagate into macroeconomic instability as prompts the notion of the supermultiplier according to which stock market shocks propagate to economic performance.

As Dividends volatility increases, Stock prices volatility decreases.

According to the supermultiplier effect the resulting economic instability will decrease.

Therefore, every thing else equal, dividend volatility should increase.

This might be achievable provided there is a relaxation of the cost of borrowing that corresponds to a better corporations' performance.

For an improved corporations' net worth the borrowers credit worthiness improves which makes them more likely to refund ther debt and benefit also from a lower borrowing rate.

Hence the ratio (Average net worth of corporations/Dividends volatility) should increase.

The prudential restriction should therefore be a ceiling on the supermultiplier ratio.

3.4 MICROPRUDENTIAL INSTRUMENTS

Adopting agreed upon profitability ranking of securities to be an essential for speculation to avoid manipulation of echoing mass purchasing and selling with bad intensions.

There should be a margin of the range of quantity of stock to be traded that is complying with the ranking of the security and a smaller margin into be subject to irrational sentiment based decision making.

This aims essentially at promoting stock market stability and resilience to contagion and badly intended speculation as a micro prudential surveillance instrument consisting in putting into equation quantity to be purchased or sold so that it is dependent up to a certain limit on rational ranking of the security and to irrational sentiment based decision making in such a way that the sentiment based decision making determines the range within which quantity traded should evolve and the median of the range is the quantity corresponding to the agreed upon ranking of the security to be determined by the prudential authority of the stock exchange board of Prudential policy makers.

The Interaction between monetary policy and stock market stability is assessed in terms of moderation of fluctuations of returns and market risk and predictability of future patterns of asset prices conditional of attenuating the volatility triggering effect of the credit and inflation transmission mechanisms of monetary policy conducting on stock prices volatility.

Instrument 1:

Dividend volatility control e(Div/MMR)

As long as according to the CAPM stock prices are inversely related to their dividends, in order to control price volatility, dividend volatility has to be controlled accurately.

This might be achieved through restricting key financially meaningful elasticity such as e(div/MMR) as indeed MMR has a role to play in setting the average loan rate or the cost of borrowing. As corporate managers proceed to an arbitrage between debt and equity financing of their production projects, it follows that the cost of borrowing is indirectly affected by book prices and dividends and also market prices that are endogenously shaped by the supply side of the firm.

As the cost of borrowing increases accordingly to a tightened monetary policy, managers of corporations increase incentives for stakeholders' to shift their financing source from debt to equity. They indeed do so continuously for the sake of the yield and profitability with the ongoing time dependent changes in the credit market conditions and monetary policy stance.

Therefore dividends are volatile. They depend on the business cycle phase; the credit market conditions the monetary policy stance and also eventually the fiscal policy.

As long as elasticity or vulnerabilities are subject to surveillance and caps, covariance between credit market conditions monetary policy stance and the volatility of stock prices in the stock market is better subjected to surveillance.

This nevertheless restricts the alternatives of corporate managers whose optimal profitability function becomes more constrained by the prudential caps or other restrictions.

Instrument 2:

- Covariance between business cycle fluctuations and stock market fluctuations:

e(average price to earnings ratio/average MBV of traded securities).

MBV is an indicator of the stance of deviation of the contribution of an individual investor from actual to potential added value.

It is consented that economic activity fluctuations and stock market values fluctuations should be cointegrated and asymptotically convergent with a lower volatility for output gap variations than market values.

As a matter of fact In the consumption based wealth model framework stock market values are ensuring from wealth in the basic asset pricing model where consumption stands for actual output level and its fluctuations stand for output gap and wealth indicates asset values.

Therefore this consumption wealth induced asset pricing model shows theoretically a co-integration between business cycle economic fluctuations and stock prices fluctuations.

We assume that the more this covariance is strong in the short and medium run the more there is threat induced by excess volatility of market prices to financial or stock market stability.

So micro prudential intervention should consider capping for an individual investor the impact of MBV on the average price to earnings ratio which serves as a gauge of the sensitivity of market volatility to business cycle fluctuations at a disaggregated level and as a gauge for avoiding that the stake of contribution of the individual investor to fluctuations of sum of added values as indicated by price to earnings ratio does not exceed the business cycle fluctuation indicator as partially correlated with MBV because market values stand for actual output whereas book values stand for potential output.

Instrument 3: The effect of investor sentiment on the cross correlation between stock prices:

e(SD average MBV/investor sentiment)

A wave of investor sentiment has larger effects on securities whose valuations are highly subjective and difficult to arbitrage. Consistent with this prediction, we find that when beginning-of-period proxies for sentiment are low, subsequent returns are relatively high for small stocks, young stocks, high volatility stocks, unprofitable stocks, non-dividend-paying stocks, extreme growth stocks, and distressed stocks. When sentiment is high, on the other hand, these categories of stock earn relatively low subsequent returns.

Classical finance theory leaves no role for investor sentiment. Rather, this theory argues that competition among rational investors, who diversify to optimize the statistical properties of their portfolios, will lead to an equilibrium in which prices equal the rationally discounted value of expected cash flows, and in which the cross-section of expected returns depends only on the cross-section of systematic risks. 1 Even if some investors are irrational, classical theory argues, their demands are offset by arbitrageurs and thus have no significant impact on prices.

Modern finance theory argues that investor sentiment may have significant effects on the cross-section of stock prices. We start with simple theoretical predictions. Because a mispricing is the result of an uninformed demand shock in the presence of a binding arbitrage constraint, we predict that a broad-based wave of sentiment has cross-sectional effects (that is, does not simply raise or lower all prices equally) when sentiment-based demands or arbitrage constraints vary across stocks. In practice, these two distinct channels lead to quite similar predictions because stocks that are likely to be most sensitive to speculative demand, those with highly subjective valuations, also tend to be the riskiest and costliest to arbitrage. Concretely, then, theory suggests two distinct channels through which the shares of certain firms—newer, smaller, more volatile, unprofitable, non-dividend paying, distressed or with extreme growth potential, and firms with analogous characteristics—are likely to be more affected by shifts in investor sentiment.

Instrument 4 : Financial accelerator control :

Ceilings on e(Div/Firm's borrowing credit worthiness) or e(Div/e(NPLs/Br))

In order to control Stock price volatility, dividend volatility has to be controlled accurately.

Borrowers' credit worthiness deteriorations or improvement bind credit conditions and cost of capital in such a way that the financial accelerator and the tradeoff between internal and external financing is affected.

As borrowers' credit worthiness varies accordingly so many criteria such as information assymetries agnecy costs, performance in past projects competition in the banking sector, nature of the investment activities of the firm if it is a targeted sector or segment of the banking sector.

By affecting the financial accelerator through borrowers' credit worthiness these factors affect the demand pull of the management team on stakeholders' supply of equity.

The more this demand pull is volatile (corresponding to supply of dividends) the more the cost push of supply of equity is volatile (corresponding to demand of dividends) the less the share price which invesely related to the dividend is volatile and the more its corresponds to resilience from excess volatility.

Therefore as sensitivity of dividends to borrowers' credit worthiness increases sensitivity of share price to borrowers' credit worthiness decreases.

Usually prevalence of circumvention information assymetries hostile business environment and alternating business cycle phases make borroswers' credit worthiness very volatile and unstable.

Therefore it is meaningful to analyse the impact effect on dividends and on share prices in order to fathom the corresponding effect on overall financial stability.

Indeed, there shold be a ceiling on sensitivity of dividends to borrowers' credit worthiness or the prevalence of a likely excess effect of variations in borrowers' credit worthiness on dividends so that share prices ought to be the least volatile preserving thereby financial stability

Instrument 5:

Cross financial sector risk mitigation sensitivity

e(hedged securities/Borrowers' credit worthiness of the corresponding corporations)

This instrument is essnetial for investors true assessment of the inherent risk pertaining to exposure to financial instability essentially because it draws a wedge between the credit sector threats that are compromisingly commingled with the stock market sector threats with respect to hedging.

Essentially hedging exacerbates financial instability for the stock market exposure to financial instability but happens to compromise in parrallel credit sector financial instability for those corporations whose securities are hedged.

Hedged securities should be very sensitive to borrowers' creditworthinesss of corporations whose securities ae hedged meaning that the more corporations are credit trust worthy in terms of borrowing the more proportions of its securitiescan be hedged without fear from compromising financial stability.

Contrariwise the less corporations are credit trustworthy meaning it has got non performing loans issues the less the proportion of its securities should be hedged sothat overall financial stability should not be hampered.

The pervasiveness of information draws a wedge between stock market valuation and assets quality.

Usually stock that performs well is backed by a good quality assets which informs on a sound management of the corporation from which the asset derives from

This means that stock that performs well enough and that does not need hedging is that which corresponds to a sound management and therefore a fairly good borrowers credit worthiness.

The rule of thumb is that if the corporation does not default with the bank it is more likely to make its shares stand for a good asset and therefore perform well and not require hedging to ensure a benefit for investors.

Instrument 6:

Supermultiplier control

Covariance between business cycle fluctuations and financial accelerator effect.

e(average price to earnings ratio/ e(Div/e(NPLs/Br)))

As the financial accelerator or the tradeoff between internal and external financing of corporations increases dividends become more sensitive to borrowers' credit worthiness. This indeed dampens the effect on share prices in terms of volatility disentangling thereby the correlation between business cycle fluctutations and the shape of share prices.

According to this effect the supermultiplier efect that translates stoch market fluctuaions in macroeconomic negative shocks is dampened an dthereby heralding less harm to the economic performance overall.

This sensitivity should decrease in order to dampen the supermultiplier effect.

There should therefore be a cap on the sensitivity of average price to earning ratio on the financial accelerator effect as average price to earning ratio is an indicator of the business cycle phase.

Indeed earning vary with respect to average price of shares in parallel to the phase cycle of the business cycle if ever the corporation economic activity is procyclical or countercyclical to the business cycle and provided it is not acyclical in order to provide a clear indication of the business cycle phase in correspondence with its varations.

4. A CONCEPTUAL MODEL OF INTEGRATION OF THE FINANCIAL SECTORS

The integration of the financial market sectors is the result of financial globalization, development accompanied by an intensification of cash flows, active innovation which is of paramount relevance specifically for the scope of this research, a growing need for efficient financial instruments and a need for risk hedging along with an accelerating interaction of international and national financial systems.

In this respect, it is needless to state that accurate consideration should be conveyed to shaping a synergistic pre-requirement of the integration process which is basically a financial sector constrained setting of a prudential framework for engineering surveillance instruments purporting at regulating in synchrony prudential restrictions for each sector.

Indeed, besides the requirement of relying on a prudential framework for the sake of mitigating the relevant market risk, this prudential framework should be shaped conditional on the side effects of other prudential frameworks relevant for other financial sectors.

As far as our research is concerned, the case under scrutiny is the synergistic pre-requirement of adapting or synchronizing Basel II and III agreements instruments of prominent relevance to the credit sector to the proposed prudential framework of surveillance in the stock market.

The prudential ratios in various financial sectors should be set conditional on accurate synchronization is adopted whenever there is conflicting effects on financial stability relative to each sector.

The prudential ratios in various financial sectors should be set conditional on accurate synchronization is adopted whenever there is conflicting effects on financial stability relative to each sector.

In the credit sector financial stability is expressed in terms of liquidity risk, credit risk, requirement risks and contagion. In the stock market sector it is expressed on implied volatility.

So whenever these elements compromise each other the relative instruments should be set conditional to each other across sectors.

Chalova, Gromova, & Voronkova (2019) introduced the concept of the "Cascade Network Modeling" of the financial market functioning, according to which, it is a potential form of its organization in which changes in the individual segments are synchronized with the purview of integrating the world financial markets or various sectors in one local financial market.

According to them: "The financial market formed in the modern economy is a unified functioning mechanism of its monetary, credit, currency, stock and insurance segments and is determined by the shared trading objects the interdependence of market institutions the interaction amog the dynamics of price indexes, the authorities regulating and the unified patterns of supply and demand generation for financial assets".

According to our view, this should be accurately shaped for the purpose of annihilating likely side effects of financial restrictions having implications that eventually offset each other whenever they are deployed simultaneously.

The prudential framework proposed to be engineered for the sake of mitigating stock market financial vulnerability and instability and its equivalent prudential framework of Basel II and III shaped for the purpose of mitigating systemic risk relative to the credit market should expand their purviews beyond the direct pre-requirements of mitigating excessive volatility which is of prominent relevance for the stock market risk and controlling liquidity risk, credit risk, capital adequacy and operational risk of prominent importance for the credit sector.

4.1. THE ISSUES OF FINANCIAL ACCELERATOR AND BORROWERS' CREDIT WORTHINESS OF CORPORATIONS

According to Fender Ingo (2000), "The concept of financial accelerator derives from informational asymmetries in the credit markets which drive a wedge between the costs of external and internal finance. In particular the higher cost of external finance reflects the agency costs of lending under asymmetric information. In such a situation internally generated funds enable firms to reduce their demand for costly external finance. Hence a fall in a borrower's net worth or cash flow raises the demand for external finance and subsequently reduces investment".

Given that negative shocks affect cash flows individually the effect of an ini-tial shock to the economy is amplified. Small shocks might therefore create large cycles hence the term financial accelerator

A contractionary monetary policy shock now reduces investment spending through the traditional cost of capital effect and given that changes in interest rates affect corporate cash flows lowers a firm's cash flow and its ability to borrow. Consequently monetary policy impulses are reinforced by cash flow effects.

In the way literature the Modigliani Miller theorem (1958) states that : « financial structure is irrelevant to corporate investment decisions ».

More recent research however has questioned the assumption of perfect substitutability of external and internal funds by pointing to the existence of capital market imperfections. The most common argument posits that asymmetric information and problems of contract enforcement lead to the emergence of agency costs thereby driving a wedge between the cost of external and internal finance. As outside investors require a premium for unobservable uncontractable risks, external finance becomes more costly than internal finance.

The issues of NPLs and Borrowers' credit worthiness is closely linked to financial stability. They bind banking sector profitability and credit risk in a fashion that triggers financial meltdowns and exacerbates economic performance slowdown.

According to Podpiera and Weil (2008) « From the 1990s up till the early 2000s a large number of banks in emerging economies collapsed owing to high non performing loans and worsened cost of efficiency.

This indeed was observed in balance sheets of banks in both emerging markets and advanced economies where NPLs were found to be major bottlenecks to their profitability ».

According to Abiola and Olausi (2014) and Richard and Al (2008) « The failure of effectively monitoring non performing loans or reduce high levels exceeding set thresholds may lead to insolvency »

Biabani and Al (2012) added "when a relatively large number of banks have NPLs surpassing their capital, banks crisis can follow which in the long run leads to a financial crisis".

Thus the root threats to financial stability from the credit sector are fathomed through a quantitative assessments of NPLs credit risk and borrowers credit worthiness at the banking sector level which lead us to adopt the perspective of the banking sector aggregates and data to assess credit worthiness rather than at the individual bank or borrower.

Dell'aricca (2001) noted that "if the banks could effectively determine the Creditworthiness of borrowers deserving borrowers could get the credit facilities thereby reducing the high rate of loan default.

Conversely an adverse selection exposure whereby high risk borrowers displace Creditworthy borrowers could cause deterioration in overall bank loan portfolio leading to a buildup of NPLs".

Borrowers' credit worthiness is defined as e(NPL/Br) where NPL stands for Non Performing loans and Br for borrowing rates.

This measure which is e(NPL/Lr) is a sound proxy for borrowers credit worthiness because it is a signal of the extent of matching between the true risk entailed by borrowers and the computed risk encompassed in risk premiums accounted for in loan rates. It measures the matching between risk premiums accounting for the risk taken into consideration by banks and the actual risk as being implicit in the measure of non performing loans.

If this elasticity increases this means that as risk premiums increase, NPLs are more sensitive to borrowing rates which makes borrowers more credit worthy and most of borrowers credit worthiness accounted for in risk premiums. Banking rating is not random or is strongly correlated with project expected profitability. Ther is precise rating and risk notation.

If this elasticity decreases this means that as risk premiums increase, NPLs are less sensitive to borrowing rates which makes borrowers less credit worthy and most borrowers credit worthiness not accounted for in risk premiums. Banking rating is random or weakly correlated with project expected profitability. There is a bad rating and risk notation.

Based on a sensitivity analysis approach, we try to interpret the sensitivity of Non performing loans to the average cost of borrowing and find out it is a fairly performing benchmark on the seriousness of the borrowers in terms of predisposition to refund the loan.

It is based on the reference in the literature about the qualification of the sensitivity of borrowers to high borrowing rates according to which borrowers should not accept high borrowing rates if not they are not willing to refund the loan.

The elasticity of non performing loans to loan rates represents an expression of the sensitivity of NPLs to loan rate increases.

It is an expression of the quality of investors selection with respect to the average cost of borrowing.

As a matter of fact, If investors are more sensitive in NPLs to increases in loan rates they are good quality investors meaning that they are not likely to incur higher borrowing costs and neglect the likelihood of non repaying their loans.

The stake of risk entailed by their financed project is accurately taken into account by the risk premium.

If investors are less sensitive in NPLs to increases in loan rates they are deemed to be bad quality investors meaning that they are likely to incur higher borrowing costs and neglect the likelihood of non repaying their loans.

The stake of risk entailed by their financed project is not accurately taken into account by the risk premium. Because of adverse selection borrowers have the tendency not repay their loans whenever borrowing rates increases do not affect their expected ability to repay the loans.

The more NPLs are elastic to borrowing rates or risk premiums the more investors are good quality investors.

This method is prospective in that it is geared toward future assessment to be valid for expectations about the impact on financial stability in the future. It is not based on historical assessments bearing information assymetries such as free riding by taking future qualifications based on past assessments although it is based on time series regressions forecasts take actual and future determinants into account in the equations.

Volatility of Dividends and stock prices and the financial accelerator :

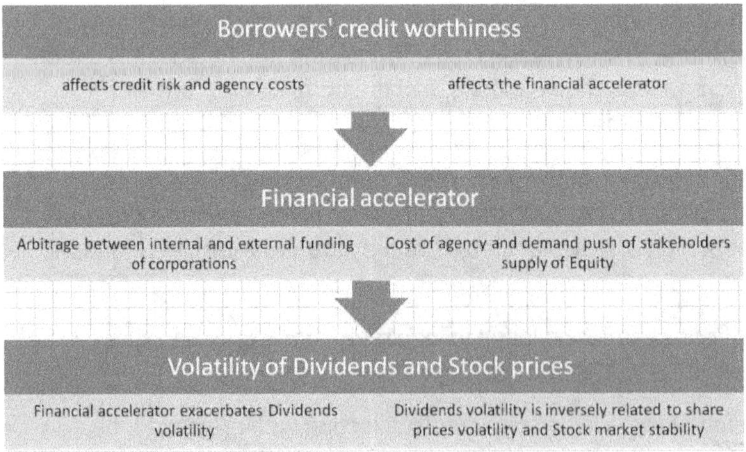

INTERPRETATION

This graphic representation shows the likages between credit sector key items of prominant relevance for credit market financial stability and key factors of prominant relevance for the Stock market financial stability which is volatility of dividends of Stock prices that according tonthe CAPM is inversely proportional to the volatility of share prices.

4.2 INVERSE PROPORTIONALITY BETWEEN SHARE PRICE VALUES AND THEIR VOLATILITY

TRANSMISSION OF CREDIT MARKET ANOMALIES TO STOCK MARKET ANOMALIES

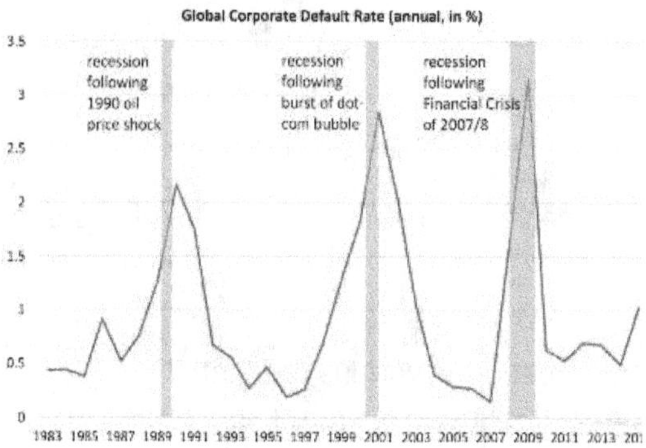

According to the graph NPLs increase drastically in global recessions. Global recessions imply essentially a sharp decline in Global Stcok market indexes.

In parallel as NPLs increase drastically, according to the financial accelerator theory implications, the arbitrage between external borrowing and equity financing implies after the sharp increase in the cost of borrowing due to degradation of borrowers' creditworthiness to a sharp increase in Risk premiums and loan rates which makes corporation managers shift to equity which includs incred volatilityof dividends and decreased volatility of share prices and hence mitigated financial instability.

This implies that when Global stock market indexes ovbserve a sharp decline stock market financial stability improves.

Contrariwise the reversal still holds ; for pikes in Global stock market indexes market risk increases drastically.

As NPLs increase the collaterals lose value MBV. Volatility of equity increases drastically.

Stock market efficiency decreases accordingly because of mismatch in market to book value far beyond the prerequisites of investor sentiment and speculation in the stock market.

Therefore non performing loans affect stock market volatility and efficiency and might herald explicitely the issue of super multiplier effect whereby volatility in stock markets translate after amplification into macroeconomic negative shocks as shown by the chart where pikes in NPLs correspond to periods of sharp recessions in the global economy after a short lag during which the transmission process of the supermultiplier occurs.

Pikes of stock market index excess volatility increases financial instability.

Throughs of stock market indexes excess volatlity decreases financial stability increases.

If we defined financial stability through excess volatility of share prices.

Hence excess volatility of share prices goes contrariwise to the value of share prices.

4.3. COLLISION AMONG INSTRUMENTS FROM DIFFERENT FINANCIAL SECTORS :

Alongside prudential restrictions collision between various prudential instruments targeting different sectors of the financial system are of commensurate importance because they play a paramount role in setting share prices of corporations.

Indeed, collision of instruments can result in either offsetting each other's prudential role or amplifying it depending on the instruments and how they interact.

These affect volatility of share prices stability of the financial sector and its efficiency which affect indirectly share prices through investor sentiment making of irrational investors and eventually arbitrage of more rational investors and thereby affect market prices.

We can propose as a case study providing an appraisal of likely threats of simultaneous deployment of restrictions in various prudential frameworks within the framework of integration; a basic scenario where LTD ratio or liquidity risk ratio and LTV ratio have conversing effects on volatility.

This indeed would provide a clear proof of the obligation of further scrutinizing cross effects between various prudential frameworks relative to various financial sectors for whom constrained optimization should be deployed to avoid that negative side effects of amplification of threats through simultaneous implementation of volatility containment and credit risk systemic exposure occurs.

First case:

This is a case of collision between the Basel III instrument of Credit market LTD with the proposed stock market surveillance instrument (Dividents/Cost of borrowing).

Capping LTD for the sake of avoiding liquidity risk in the credit market results in a relative excess generated in credit demand. The excess in credit demand is eventually according to the basic supply and demand theory met by an excess supply. But as long as there is a LTD restriction, that would translate by higher average loan rates.

Management of corporations operates a continuous arbitrage for the sake of minimizing the cost of capital. It proceeds to an arbitrage between the cost of equity and the cost of debt to assess whether their operational projects or expansions should be debt or equity financed.

The increase in average loan rates would exert an effect on this arbitrage making the demand for equity higher, fact that would put an upward pressure on dividends prices.

Depending on the business cycle phase and the resulting expected profitability of the corporations production activities, the effect of increasing average loan rates on dividends would fluctuate accordingly which generates a certain business cycle dependent volatility that translates accordingly to share prices and contributes in increasing share prices volatility and the overall volatility of the stock market.

Therefore, this case is an instance where deploying LTD restrictions in the credit market translates into an excess volatility in the stock market and compromises stock market systemic vulnerability.

To avoid that synchronization failures across various prudential surveillance frameworks occur, the LTD ratio should be set constrained in optimization by the requirement of offsetting the detrimental effect on excess volatility of dividends.

Second case:

The second case of collision is that between LTV ratio as a Basel III instrument and the stock market surveillance instrument (Tangible assets/Equity).

LTV restrictions are mainly caps on LTV ratios.

We propose to study the effect of its variations on the book to market value of stock.

The prudential restriction in the credit market consists in lowering average LTV ratios which depresses property values.

Depressing property values by exerting a downward pressure on their prices will expand the discrepancy between market values and book values of shares.

As a matter of fact, among corporate assets, tangible assets are mainly property assets of corporations. So whenever their market value is depressed the tangible assets have lower value and so does the book or accounting value of the firm.

By a way of consequence, the difference between the market value and the book value of the firm is wider.

According to the review of the literature, there is a close relationship between stock market efficiency and market to book value from one side and an inverse relationship between market efficiency and market stability from the other.

This implies mainly that wider difference between book and market values of the firm exert a negative effect on stock market efficiency and by a way of consequence a positive effect on stock market stability.

So for this case, the effect of the implementation of the credit market prudential restriction on stock market stability is an amplification or a positive side effect whereby proceeding to mitigating credit market risk contributes in mitigating stock market risk.

4.3 THE BALANCED SCORECARD AND ITS IMPLICATION ON THE INTEGRATION OF FINANCIAL SECTORS

The Balanced ScoreCard is a key concept for the integration of financial sectors.

According to Abdali (2013) « The integration between performance and risk management enables organizations to both monitor and evaluate the performance effectually through the balanced scorecard and to prevent further unfavorable consequences resulting from uncertain performance ».

Gordona Loeba and Tsengb (2009) discussed the newtrend in viewing the risk management. They noticed the new trend of holistic view of risk management which is commonly referred to as entreprise risk management (ERM).

According to them : « Five factors have an impact on the ERM. These factors are ; the environmental uncertainty, the industy competition, the firm complexity, and its size and the Board of directors' monitoring »

These factors fall into the scope of rational assessment of investment by traders in the secondary market.

Their assessment is intended to depict expected beneficial investment opportunities and does affect fluctuations of the Stock market index with pikes and troughs.

But, as far as financial stability pertaining to the stock market is concerned, it still stands that the key factor or criterion of prominant relevance for excess volatility of the Stock market index which is compromising for financial stability is the cross correlation between share prices which is not available in the BSC. Nonetheless the BSC can provide a clue about the patterns of the Stock market index and henceforth through the diversification of trading forthe sake of disentangling the traders from the commmonly followed behavior that binds the average trend of the stock index.

This has the effect of dumpening excess volatility up to a certain limit.

Bu it is yet uncertain how far does the portfolio diversification of rational investors affect excess fluctuations and how far it affects excess volatility.

Anyway the BSC is expected to provide a clear assessment of expected risk and uncertainty about future corporations performance financially and non financially.

As far as the BSC is concerned Beasley, Chen Nunez and Wright (2006) put an emphasis on the potential benefits of developing a set key risk indicator KRI.

They stated that : « The potential value of KRI may be derived from different contributions such as risk appetite by determining an appropriate threshold for action at different organisations levels. Risk and opportunity identified by designing KRIs to alert management to trends that may affect the achievement of organisational objectives or may introduce new opportunities. Risk treatment by serving mechanisms for organisational units and Risk reporting by providing measurable data conclusive to aggregation »

These features fall Into the scope of annihilating the cross correlation among share prices as they display for the trader the required tools to diversify his trading strategy sothat it gets disentangled from mass comparable trading strategies that not only motivate cross correlations among share prices but also minimise expected earnings as they are shared opportunities rather than innovations in depicting favorable opportunities most expected to be beneficial.

The BSC draws a wedge between unveiling the risk management root items and hence the creditworthiness of the corporation into consiederation and its effect or contribution in credit risk or risk of non performing loans for the credit sector which is a building block of financial instability from the standpoint of the credit sector and the rational information gathering sources for traders in the Stock market that involves efficiency and stability as reviewed in section 2 whereby efficiency of the stock market is related to its stability.

Nevertheless it still stands that financial stability ffrom the stock market perspective is compromised by excess volatility of stock prices whose fluctuations are essentially due to cross correlated stocks i.e stocks that vary in the same direction once a perturbance occurs.

Besides basically financial stability from the stock market standpoint is threatened by irrationally based trading or trading that is more likely to be beneficial and lead to a bandwagon effect of following up or what we might call a speculative attack that compromises tremendoussly stock market stability.

The balanced scorecard affects considerably the MBV and by of consequence Stock market efficiency.

It is also obvious that it affects excess volatility of share prices even if there are claims that investor trading patterns are driven byvsentiment and irrationally cast patterns of purchasing and selling of Stock.

The BSC ensures that an adequate assessment of risk aspects pertaining to corporations can exhibit future patterns of profitability and by a way of consequence make information accessible to traders more adequate and less assymetric fact that ensures least volatility in face of clear foresightedness of future profitability expectations.

Thus affordability of a reliable balanced scorecard in itself can helpnmitigate financial.instability provided the irrationality of traders is rational up to a certain point which is not guaranteed.

As a matter of fact, disrespectfully of the fact that the risk assessment of an entrepreneurial activity of a quoted corporation is trivial for financial stability pertaining to the Stock market sector it still stands of commensurate relevance for financial stability considerations pertaining to the credit sector.

Indeed, borrowers' credit worthiness and credit scoring which are of prominant relevance for credit risk assessed by banks, the BSC provides key information of prominant relevance for unveiling uncertainty for risk assessment by the credit sector.

By a way of consequence the assessment of borrowers' credit worthiness becomes more accurate and credit risk which is proportional to financial instability is attenuated.

The interaction between the stock market sector and the credit sector is better fathomed once we settle an accurate and precise BSC.

This is essentially due to the fact that rational assessment of corporations by traders in the stock market goes in parrallel with the corporations solvency and its credit worthiness vis à vis-à-vis the bank or the loan supplier which affects financial instability of the credit sector and eventually borrowing costs subject to risk premiums assessments.

Excess volatility of stock prices results from cross correlations between stock prices fluctuations and not excess risk entailed by the corporations operations.

As long as risk is taken into consideration especially if it is clearly specified In the balance scorecard investor trading behavior becomes rational subject to objective assessment.

By a way of consequence earnings prospects are attenuated considerably except for those investment opportunities that surprise the market.

Indeed these beneficial trading opportunities cannot be involving the concern of rationally guided investors that analyse objectively their investment opportunities based on available information including the balance scorecard.

Nevertheless it still stands that the better shaped is the BSC the closer is the MBV (market to book value) to 1 and the the more efficient is the stock market.

5. HEDGING AND THE BALANCED SCORECARD: AN APPRAISAL REGARDING STABILITY

5.1. THE IMPORTANCE OF HEDGING FOR STABILITY

According to Fender (2000), "Derivatives enable their users to separate value and transfer market risks. Risks are securitized and thus gain fungibility which in turn allows the unbundling and repackaging of market risks embodied in underlying assets. The use of derivatives therefore enhances the possibilities for active corporate risk management which is likely to have an impact on macroeconomic and monetary issues".

The threat from derivatives to stock market stability comes from the financial accelerator.

Indeed, by hedging interest rates, the wedge between internal and external financing for corporations vanishes. Therefore, equity becomes less necessary. Hence, stakeholders exert less power and become by a way of consequence less sensitive to projects outcomes. Therefore, dividends are less volatile and so are stock prices, what proves that derivatives are a main cause for stock market stability.

By ensuring more stability they compromise efficiency.

Therefore, there are two opponent views on the way derivatives affect stock market stability.

Information asymmetries and the skepticism about Modigliani's theory raises a concern about how far the credit channel of transmission of monetary policy does affects stock prices volatility.

In terms of integration must of portraying a prudential scheme and rendering interaction across financial sectors permissible, the stock market sector presents the specificity of encompassing a stock options feature that compromises the purview of the true scope of the key market risk fundamental which is volatility on which we based our fundamental justification of market risk and that does not hold in this instance.

According to Sajjad and Zamman: "Derivatives enable firms to hedge against systemic risks".

As long as prudential surveillance is related to systemic risk mitigation, it follows that hedging does play a prudential role of hedging against systemic risks and financial instability as much as prudential instruments like the ones displayed in the framework of the engineering we proceeded to in this article.

Indeed, as long as stock options cancel any possibility of loss, excess volatility does no longer imply necessarily as a main cause for market risk and instability.

The basic framework set sofar does no longer hold and requires further extensions concerning either the concepts of efficiency or stability which reveal a compromising further purview in terms of prudential surveillance instruments engineering.

It is considered that derivatives increase the efficiency of the financial system. By a way of consequence they deteriorate stability.

Here surges a conundrum whereby from one side derivatives hedge from losses and by a way of consequence market risk and from the other side by deteriorating stability they call the urge for further Prudential intervening. But as long as the most prominent role of prudential intervention is ensuring more stability. It is consented that prudential instruments are mainly purporting at mitigating the very source of market risk which is excess volatility.

But given the nature of hedging of derivatives, excess volatility does not necessarily compromise market risk for investors in the sense of presenting a source of loss.

So where does the threat from derivatives to stability really come from?

Corporate hedging affects directly Stock market stability through the risk management related issue affecting equity and henceforth valuation either book or market one and indirectly observable through the balanced scorecard that provides enough information to judge on whether the firm is credit worthy compromises the credit risk of the credit market and threatens of future non performing loans as the BSC justifies future prospects of the organisation that are not necessarily of financial nature but at least of prominant relevance for the assessment of probability of default.

Basically, the issues of stability promotion and efficiency improvement are contradictory and represent a conundrum because on the one hand; they are both of paramount importance what means that there is a need for promoting stability of the stock market and simultaneously improving efficiency in the sense of Pareto optimality.

On the other hand; with an efficient stock market book values converge to market values because efficiency is bound to Pareto optimality what means we cannot improve the situation of one agent or investor without deteriorating the situation or expected earnings of the other.

Indeed, in this case, stability of the stock market does not hold because with attenuation of information asymmetries that deepen the gap between book values and market values of stock, prices volatility of stocks increases considerably with increasing correlations between stock prices in similar entrepreneurial activities.

This in turn deteriorates stability with increased covariance between stock prices volatility is increased considerably.

But it is possible for stability promotion and efficiency of allocation in the Pareto sense hypotheses to hold simultaneously in the case of the introduction of derivatives.

As long as hedging assumes guaranteeing absence of losses for a part of investors so by hedging we break the pattern of volatility and covariance between stock prices whenever hedging in itself is not systemic or does not hold for all similar stock securities.

So we will find a scenario where stability is improved and also efficiency is improved because efficiency is based on convergence between book and market values if stock prices what would require attenuation of information asymmetries. This feature is mostly subject to improvement in the case of hedging where information about expected returns is better affordable by investors that ensure impossibility of incurring losses.

In definitive, using hedging derivatives resolves the conundrum of having both musts of promoting stability and improving efficiency.

Yet, according to another view, it is commonly argued in literature on the impact of derivatives on stock market efficiency that derivatives promote stock market efficiency and outcome on stock market stability is suggestible to many skeptical views as to whether it is positive or negative.

Indeed, by induction, as long as the impact of derivatives on efficiency is positive and that it is consented in the referred to literature that efficiency is inversely related to stability, this holds for both stock market analytics and banking system analytics, then the impact on stock market stability should be negative.

But from another standpoint taking into consideration the effect of derivatives on the agency problems and the fact that the financial accelerator theory contradicts the Modigliani Miller theorem, there are cases where indeed, adopting derivatives leads to a situation where both effects on efficiency and stability of the stock market are positive.

For further scrutiny of this case, let us consider that usually stakeholders have a certain supply power of internal sources of financing and that due to this power, their sensitivity to affordable information about the future outcome of projects either expansionary or development projects varies accordingly to their power. Henceforth, the effect of an increase in elasticity due to increased power as external financing is higher than internal financing because agency problems lead their dividends to be highly volatile. As dividends are highly volatile and inversely proportional to stock prices, it follows that stock prices are also highly volatile which is detrimental to stock market stability.

But as for our instance the introduction of derivatives as an option for corporate managers expands the purview of predictability of cash flows it provides by a way of consequence more accurate information which decreases agency problems in such a way that attenuates the discrepancies between the cost of external and internal financing.

In this special case, the power stakeholders exert on corporate management decreases and so does their elasticity of supply of funds. Therefore dividends are less volatile and so are stock prices.

In definitive, this is the case where the option of buying derivatives by corporate managers leads to less volatile stock prices and hence enhanced stock market stability once the issue is aggregated from the individual firm level to the stock market level.

In this case, both effects of introducing derivatives on stock market efficiency and stability are positive.

Dodd discussed in depth the issue of the effect of derivatives on financial markets and came out to a conclusion that basically derivatives improve stability and efficiency provided by certain conditions on exchange markets.

Dodd (2002) stated that: "Derivatives play a double role in an economy; one of which is economically useful role played in hedging and risk management and enables capital inflows to developing countries; and the other is the role of price discovery and establishment of standard market prices that helps reduce uncertainty and promotes stability and efficiency of the market".

But Dodd (2000) stated that: "Derivatives can play a significant role in the creation of financial crises if conditions of speculation exist. He further noted that during possible reduction of currency costs after getting to a profitable exchange position an attack toward fixed or floating exchange rate regime indicates the creation of a crisis. Thus systemic risk is created in financial markets and the tendency of contagion across countries increases. In conclusion financial markets with derivatives can become ineffective because of speculative attacks on exchange rate variations of positions".

5.2. THE PRUDENTIAL ROLE PLAYED BY HEDGING

The issue of prudential surveillance is especially concerned by the use of derivatives.

As a matter of fact; on the one hand by improving efficiency and stability the use of hedging instruments alleviate burdens on the task of prudential surveillance by making it easier to promote financial stability and efficiency; but on the other hand by helping create crises and increasing systemic risk in the case of speculation and speculative attacks on exchange positions the use of derivatives worsens the situation and urges the call for contagion targeting prudential instruments.

Hedging does play a macro prudential role by capping the riskiness of expected returns that are fundamental in increasing volatility of stock returns.

As a matter of fact, volatility of stock returns is the core source of systemic risk in stock market as it is pro cyclical with its own industry average beha-vior of returns and the business cycle and determines the pattern of sys-temic exposure of the stock market because stock returns determine stock prices.

So by hedging we break the pattern of volatility and covariance between stock prices whenever hedging in itself is not systemic or does not hold for all similar stock securities.

Certainly hedging plays a macro prudential role but cannot be taken for a macro prudential instrument as it is not intended at mitigating financial vulnerability but at ensuring minimizing losses on returns.

As long as the objectives of hedging and prudential surveillance are different they cannot be taken for holding as fulfilling the same task.

5.3 HEDGING AND THE BALANCED SCORE CARD

Hedging is about a financial stategy of derivatives that derives from conventional financial instruments that uses financial instruments or market strategies to offset the risk of any adverse price movements.

Investors hedge one investment by making a trade in another.

In pure economic terms, this introduces frictions that display merits in terms of expectations and probabilities of earnings for investors as it works as a warranty for shielding from losses.

But these frictions will essentially lead through contagion to a bad quality of assets whereby corporations hedging for the outcome of acquisitions and transactions that are quoted in the stock market are likely not to care about a criterion that affects tremendously the cost of borrowing which is the analogous source of financing for equity.

At this stage it is noteworthy that by recoursing to hedging we neglect the balanced scorecard suggestions about risk management as earnings are guaranteed disrespectfully of the assessment of risk and the organisational hindrances to performance iprovements that might exacerbate borrowers' credit worthiness and the probability of non performing loans.

Henceforth this will introduce of bias of selecton and exacerbate the financial stability of the credit market.

Indeed as long as the corporation assets are hedged against future losses it will matter least for the corporation management if the cost of external borrowing is minimised. This will affect negatively borrowers' credit worthiness as the corporation management will no longer care about the way the financial intermediary which is the bank will shed the light on their probability of default or what could be called their borrowers 'credit worthiness. Besiides they will neglect the balanced scorecard supervision advices about risk managment and organisational implications on performance.

This will introduce an information assymetry which is adverse selection and will lead the corporation to have a misconduct about expansion projects appraisal and risk of default which will exacerbate financial stability from the credit sector side.

The pervasiveness of information draws a wedge between stock market valuation and assets quality.

Usually stock that performs well is backed by a good quality assets which informs on a sound management of the corporation from which the asset derives from

This means that stock that performs well enough and that does not need hedging is that which corresponds to a sound management and therefore a fairly good borrowers credit worthiness.

The rule of thumb is that if the corporation does not default with the bank it is more likely to make its shares stand for a good asset and therefore perform well and not require hedging to ensure a benefit for investors.

So in definitive although hedging exerts a positive effect on Stock market financial stability it does exert a negative effect on credit market financial stability.

Ther is a skepticism about its overall effect as it is tough to weigh the effect of warranting expected future losses in the stockmarket with the effect of a deterioration in borrowers' credit worthiness and the probability of default on loans which is very harmful in terms of financil stability.

6. THE CONUNDRUM OF EFFICIENCY AND STABILITY OF THE STOCK MARKET

We propose to prove that stability is conversial to efficiency in two various ways for the stock market sector and that for the credit sector stability varies in the same way as efficiency but in opposite direction with effectivenss.

It is noteworthy to remind that trading in the stock market is either rational based on considerations of the financial situation of corporations or on their balanced scorecard or automated based on alghorytmic trading or depiction of incremental symptoms of improvements in earnings expectations or irrationally founded based on betting and heards in speculation.

In structure, trading occurs in the primary or in the secondary market.

We are concerned with trading taking place in the secondary market for academic analyses purposes in order to avoid commingling the primary market where investment banks complicate the stock market analysis with a must of being concerned with the credit market considerations and other banking assets profitability considerations (ROA) in their balance sheets.

So we skip the primary market for simplification concerns.

These three types of trading in the secondary market bear consequences of prominent relevance for the matter of stability and efficiency of the stock market and obviously compromise the must of ensuring resilience from financial instability and the interaction process across financial sectors up to a certain limit.

6.1 RATIONALLY BASED TRADING IN THE SECONDARY MARKET

Rationally based trading is commonly adopted and quite straightforward in that it does not compromise financial stability because of predictability of patterns of evolution based on rationally set criteria of assessment such as financial reports cash flow statements or the balanced scorecard.

These indeed not only do not leave room for excess covariance betwen stcok returns which is compromising for financial stability but are acccompained with minimal benefits as those statements are available information for the public and hence abide any innovation of grasping a distinct trading opportunity that enables to reap a beneficial reward in terms of trading.

6.2 ALGORYTMIC TRADING AND SPECULATION IN THE SECONDARY MARKET

An appraisal of the operational method of alghorytmic trading and speculation shows that while alghorytmuc trading enhances stability and deteriorates efficiency, speculation enhances efficiency and deteriorates stability because of excess correlation and hearding of stock prices and the increased likelihood of highly correlated implications of echoing winning speculation

Alghorytmic trading uses complicated mathematics with a high probability and low expectation of earnings but does not ensure a good earning like speculation based on investor sentiment for which profits have low probability and high expectations.

Alghorytmic trading as being based on advanced mathematical calculus dissipates mass invesment probability by depicting at high frequency instercies and by a way of consequence decrease the probability of high cross correlation of stock prices that leads to excess fluctuation of the stock market indexes. Therefore it enhances financial stability while at the same time does not optimalise efficiency.

6.3 THE IMPLICATIONS OF EFFICIENCY HYPOTHESES ON FINANCIAL STABILITY

Efficiency of equilibrium in the stock market is measured in terms of market value premium over book value. This means essentially that stock market efficiency is inversely proportional to its stability.

The hindrance of gathering both efficiency and stability in the stock market raises the debate of incompatibility between prudential aspects and efficiency aspects in equilibrium.

Prudential surveillance should be constrained by the task of favoring an optimal efficient market value of stocks if not the distortions introduced by Prudential instruments become too expensive for stock market efficiency considerations and for the effect of efficiency of the stock market on economic performance.

The efficiency hypothesis assuming Pareto optimality holds that we cannot improve the profitability prospects of an investor or a trader without deteriorating the profitability of another trader.

Investors have the tendency to look for new comers newly securitised, Information Technology and Research and Development firms or firms that are under restructuring and financial distress, in order to ascertain predictable pattern of trading prices which is difficult to forecast for coportations with historical data and balance sheets affordable to all traders. Therefore, and because usually there exists a high cross correlation among the price volatility of these types of securities that are either financially distressed or new comers and research firms with longitudinal expectations of non linear earnings that begin negative then jump to extremely profitable ubruptly, financial stability is harmed by trading in cross correlated securities patterns that increases volatility of share prices and excaerbates financial instability.

6.4 RATIONAL, ALGHORYTMIC TRADING, SPECULATION AND FINANCIAL STABILITY Alghorytmic trading as well as intentional isolated betting can lead to a speculative attack.

The hindrance to stock market stability is more severe with alghorytmic trading but rare because with alghorytmic trading there are no heards and news of prominant relevance that lead traders to follow collectively in a pervasive way because of shortage in information of prominant relevance.

But in the case of betting the sequence of trading is so isolated that traders think reliable information is available for a set of investors and that this trading should be followed collectively blindly taking into account the search for yield motivation of the betters who become very easily influencable by their reaction to other traders behavior through imitation because they are not motivated by rational analyses that lesses their influence by other traders.

Therefore, the expectation of speculative attacks due to betting is high but its variance is low because as long as betting is intentional traders are not driven by automated mechanisms and can cancel the pattern they basically tried to follow to take advantage of a likely opportunity.

For the case of prudential intervention set in analogy with the Basel IV framework of sensitivity based approach ;

The speculation induced volatility is measured in terms of covariance between share prices.

Or eventually the sensitivity of covariance between share prices to the regulatory benchmark.

The highest expectations have necessarily the lowest variations and correspond to betting and the lowest expectations have the highest variations and correspond to alghorytmic trading.

The threat obviously comes from alghorytmic trading and therefore is systemic because of the pervasiveness of alghorytmic trading with respect to randomness of betting.

7. CONCLUSION

Investor risk appetite as being inversely proportional to the principal component of market indicators fathoming the general tendency of market fluctuations is seemingly stimulated during tranquil periods of volatility.

Systemic risk is therefore pervasive in the meaning it is either excess volatility borne or investor behavior born.

In either cases, the efficient market hypothesis that does not hold as according to the literature holds as a main source of overshooting and undershooting that further exacerbate the market risk and motivate the paramount importance of setting a prudential framework with its both aspects.

The macroprudential instruments are expected to regulate the market risk aspect whereas the microprudential instruments are expected to regulate the individual investor hindrance to financial stability.

Both aspects commingle to set a prudential surveillance framework aiming at containing the threats to financial stability.

Additional aspects of integration of financial sectors such as collision among instruments, the effects of Balanced Score Card are of prominant relevance for the financial stability considerations especially if the notions of Non Performing Loans Borrowers credit worthiness and information assymetries are introduced. It then becomes obvious how financila stability in the banking sector affects through feed back loop through the financial accelerator thefinancial stability in the Stock market sector .

Within the scope of the newly engineered stock market Prudential toolkit, the macroprudential instruments that have been proposed as taking ratio forms imposing regulations in caps or ceilings are: the cost of capital ratio, the volatility induced allocation of equity, the countercyclical financial accelerator buffers and the sensitivity of stakeholders to profitability of companies.

For the microprudential toolkit instruments are taking the form of elasticities such as dividend volatility control instrument, the covariance between business cycle fluctuations and stock market fluctuations and the effect of investor sentiment on the cross correlation between stock prices.

All these proposed instruments are assumed to unveil major hindrances to financial instability stemming from stock prices excess volatility and to provide comprehensive surveillance reinvigorating the Basel framework that has been specific to mitigating the credit sector threats to financial stability with a pervasively prevailing threat to financial stability stemming from the stock market sector.

Hedging plays a prominant role for prudentiality and while being beneficial to the stock market financial stability compromises the credit market financial stability.

Trading in the secondary market is mainly either based on rationality, pure betting or alghorytmic trading and displays varying implications on financial stability accordingly.

Part III

THEORETICAL NOTIONS OF FINANCIAL SECTOR RISK AND THE BASEL FRAMEWORKS

Keywords:

Risk moments, Dispersion, Early warning, Borrowers' creditworthiness, Investor risk appetite, Balanced Score Card, Information asymmetries, Hedging, Convergence, Gravitation, instability across financial sectors

Abstract:

This part discusses financial stability related notions of risk, the issue of convergence and cross financial sector prudential intervention.

It elucidates the Basel framework shortcomings and enunciates the requirement of setting a reinvigorated prudential framework before proceeding to its essentials in terms of engineering.

It highlights an early warning approach dealing with the issue of time reaction mismatch of the prudential authority and the priority of setting a long run forwarded guided approach.

The objective of this research is to provide a clue into enhancing prudential setting of instruments, the forwardedly guided purview of surveillance as well as hedging and the Balanced Score Card.

1. Introduction

The Basel framework in all its versions tried to tackle the issue of prudential surveillance and to find a way out of systemic exposure for the credit market. It is accountable for many improvements in terms of resilience from risk root items and the outburst of financial meltdowns but still remains with many shortcomings that have to be annihilated in order to ascertain complete resilience. One first step to achieve this goal is to criticize accurately the Basel framework and show explicitly its shortcomings for the sake of finding an end to them. While ascertaining to accomplish this endeavoring task we find theoretical evidence of a prominent role played by items exerting cross effects among financial sectors such as Risk moments Risk dispersion over time, and henceforth early warning systems, the issues of NPLs, Borrowers creditworthiness, Information asymmetries and so on. This been said as long as stock market sector stability matters a lot for overall financial stability; it still stands that the issue of hedging raises a debate of having to face complicated ordeals having cross effects that reveal controversial as their implications require choice of priorities in situations where accomplishment of all alternatives is a must to ensure adequate resilience from risk hindrances root causes, the onslaught of financial meltdowns and improved performance of the financial sectors simultaneously whenever the situation of one is compromising for the situation of the other as is clearly obvious. In this chapter we raise numerous issues related to financial instability mitigation prerequisites and try to provide adequate answers to them.

Is the Basel IV framework based on sensitivity analyses a good fit for an upgrading of conventional prudential surveillance? What instruments grasp most the basics of threats accompanying uncertainty, excessive fluctuations of equity prices and systemic market risk? Is a new structural expression of Risk needed to better grasp its key features and afford its supervision and does it sketch to finance theory implications as to principles of dispersion? How do main features characterizing the credit sector such as information asymmetries Non performing loans and borrowers' credit worthiness affect share prices volatility thereby exacerbating financial stability and the propagation of risk root items across financial sectors? Is there a need for adopting long run prudential surveillance grasped by what we would call early warning? What are the prerequisites for ensuring a best forecasting of long run relationships or jump effects in terms of prudentiality? What specific role is played by hedging in terms of prudentiality for both the credit sector and the stock market sector? The conventional macro prudential framework of surveillance assumes implicitly that is sufficient to promote financial stability for the overall financial system and mitigate related financial vulnerabilities and risk. These assertions should be subjected to strong criticism as stock market risk stands for a financial instability driver as much as the credit market. Besides what complicates further the endeavor of ensuring awareness and resilience of the banking system is that it is not sufficient to make other financial sectors fit the financial instability mitigation prerequisites and that indeed the various financial sectors interact with each other with many respects. Here the issues of non performing loans information asymmetries and borrowers credit worthiness along with hedging further complicate the analysis and generates externalities or side effects that might reveal being problematic in that they raise a controversial interrogation on the stake of efficiency and stability in ensuring complete resilience and accurate performance of both financial sectors. The perspective of risk mitigation should encompass risk mitigation of economic projects. Alongside risk mitigation of risk coming from liquidity and credit risk from the banking perspective and excess volatility and hedging deteriorating consequences coming from trading of securities, it is clear that a perspective directed towards economic and business projects where project risk is divided into equity relative risk and external borrowing relative risk grasps the credit risk pertaining to the banking sector and one part of volatility in the share prices coming from disinformativeness with respect to share prices and profitability outcomes pertaining to the stock market sector. In this respect the dispersion of risk measured by its variance, the moments which are skew and curtosis of risk matter far more than barely limiting prudential intervention to banking and stock market supervision. There should be room to target framing variance of risk in such a way that makes early warning easier for clear-sightedness of future hindrances to systemic risk mitigation. Furthermore, as credit and liquidity risks are generally subjected to jump effects that herald unexpectedly, it is obviously of commensurate importance to go deep inside the likelihood of having regime switching models that describe at best over the long run the behavior of items related to systemic exposure such as credit risk or liquidity risk or illiquidity risk. Besides information asymmetries and inefficiency result in generation of risks as they are structural market imperfections that exacerbate the prevalence of conjectural hindrances such as credit risk and excess volatility of share prices in the credit market and stock market respectively. In the following, we will deal with each issue separately with full consideration of their interlink ages and implications on each other.

2. A NEW COMPOSITION OF RISK AND A BINDING CONDITION FOR RISK DISTRIBUTION IN COMPLIANCE WITH FINANCE THEORY

2.1 COMPOSITION OF RISK

In the literature on Risk and credit risk, the usually adopted Risk composition is about idiosyncratic risk and systemic risk.

We assume with reference to Frei (2017), that Risk comprises three main components.

-The point in time component which involves subjection to cyclicality and autocorrelation.

-The stable component or through the cycle component which involves innovation due to industrial specificities.

-The uncertainty component which is exclusively tributary to uncertainty and is neither subject to cyclicality nor to industry specificities and is distinguished by asymptotic un-correlation and asymptotic neglectibility of innovations.

This composition displays the feature of disentangling the aspects depictable through prudential restrictions from those subjectable to probabilistic assessments and those retraceable with business cycle related analyses,

As a matter of fact uncertainty should be subjected to probabilistic assessments whereas through the cycle aspects should be targeted through prudential restrictions and point in time risk can be traced back by comparing its pattern to that of OG within the framework of business cycle analyses.

Risk mitigation involves being cautious about financial stability which grasps its main drawbacks on the financial system.

Risk implies financial vulnerability and instability and is assumed to harm the entire financial system in such a way it might trigger a financial meltdown whenever excessive .

Uncertainty and the search for yield generate risk that is mainly harmful for the banking and the stock market sector although it might be beneficial as long as it is bound to profitability.

This issue has been delt with within the framework of the Basel frameworks and stock market prudential regulation as documented in Basel II through IV. But a lot has still to be achieved and reinvigorated under the scope of these purviews to afford better resilience from Risk and its implications.

Hedging from risk in the financial system cannot be ascertained because Hedging in the stock market is compromisingly involving the credit sector in excess risk and Hedging in the credit market which is claimed to be deployed through implementation of prudential restrictions as it amplifies excess volatility of share prices.

2.2 RISK MOMENTS AND PRUDENTIAL SURVEILLANCE

Among the main shortcomings of the Basel frameworks stands the fact that its scope is to mitigate risk disrespectfully of its composition in structure but taking into account solely its nature either liquidity risk or credit risk or capital non adequacy.

But there should be room for consideration of moments of risk under the scope of risk supervision either ex-post for static risk assessment or ex-ante for early warning forecasting as risk is a random variable and the more it is dispersed in probability of occurrence the more it is unpredictable hence not subject to accurate framing and not accounted for in a precise way.

Thus a more appropriate goal for prudential surveillance should be risk moments framing and restrictions alongside mitigation of expectation of risk.

The perspective of risk mitigation should encompass risk mitigation of economic projects.

Alongside risk mitigation of risk coming from liquidity and credit risk from the banking perspective and excess volatility and hedging deteriorating consequences coming from trading of securities, it is clear that a perspective directed towards economic and business projects where project risk is divided into equity relative risk and external borrowing relative risk grasps the credit risk pertaining to the banking sector and one part of volatility in the share prices coming from disinformativeness with respect to share prices and profitability outcomes pertaining to the stock market sector.

In this respect, the moments of risk matter far more than its expectation provided risk is taken for a random variable.

There should be room to target a concise framing of risk moments for forecasting purposes as a prudential surveillance approach aiming at mitigating financial instability and vulnerability in a more concise way rather than solely mitigating risk.

Risk scoring should be proceeded to in function of all Risk moments, Mean, variance, skew and Kurtosis together with higher moments VAR value at risk and CVAR conditional value at risk and not only expectation and overall probability of occurrence.

It should be dynamic or time dependent in that it encompasses future Risk prospects ex-ante in function of early warning modeling.

If not Risk restriction lacks of accuracy and precision.

Hence prudential surveillance should focus on all Risk moments rather than barely Risk expectation.

This should be conducted disrespectfully of the fact that risk moments are endogenous in nature and that they are pertaining to projects being financed for the banking sector and equities being listed in the stock market sector.

In this respect, prudential surveillance has got the tools to restrict the banking and stock market intermediation but cannot restrict the risk tails and moments that are tributary to projects and equities independent from the service being provided by a bank or a stock market trading.

Prudential surveillance can mitigate risk assuming it displays features controlling its determinants.

It is easily proven that prudential surveillance can control contagion liquidity risk credit risk capital adequacy and excess volatility of stock markets.

But is it likely to affect the risk distribution and its moments? Can it affect the risk skew and Kurtosis and higher moments like Value at risk and conditional Value at risk?

It is consented that Variance Skew and Kurtosis are endogenous to risk tails.

Papers referring to the four moments optimization for risk return optimization which are Mean or expectation, Variance Skew and Kurtosis are like Harvey (2003), Kenalbay Ozut and Franko (2011), Beardsley Field and Xiao (2012), Saranya and Prasanna (2014), and Harvey Liechty , Liechty and Muller (2013).

As far as prudential surveillance is concerned and due to the fact that risk moments are endogenous to risk and cannot be restricted by a financial intermediaries, we state that the BSC, the auditing techniques and technical advising can help affect risk tails commensurately.

A comprehensive methodology of intervention proceeded by central banking and industry authorities can help limit and mitigate risk tails commensurately by reversing abnormal patterns by key entrepreneurial intervenient that might exhibit abnormal investment decision that translate into more imprudent risk tails in vertical integration through contagion.

In industries correlated vertically the risk incurred by the supplier is incurred by the retailer with an add up and propagation of risk biased by correlated patterns of skew and kurtosis.

Through the adequate fine tuning of the Balanced Score Cards and advising centralized at the relevant authorities of industry and Central Banking, there is room for containing abnormal behavior of risk tails that might exacerbate systemic exposure through adjustment of cross correlation among vertically linked industrial and commercial activities as well as uncertainty related to risk variance and its moments; skew and Kurtosis.

This can be adopted through benchmarking of similarity with observed risks dispersion from historical Balanced Score cards of enterprises as well as available performance of credit worthiness and risk scoring from the banking system and some past observations of share price evolutions and adjustments of accounting performance of listed enterprises to their market performance that are assumed to allow to go deeper into details and specificities of past risk tails

2.3 A MATHEMATICAL PROOF OF THE PREVAILANCE OF A POLYNOMIAL STRUCTURE OF VARIANCE OF RISK UNDER DYNAMIC DISTRIBUTION AND UNCERTAINTY

Sheng and Yao (2014) stated about chance theory that: "Uncertainty and randomness are two basic types of indeterminacy. Chance theory was founded for modeling complex systems with not only uncertainty but also randomness. There are some important characteristics about uncertain random variables; the expected value is the average value of uncertain random variable in the sense of chance measures and represents the size of uncertain random variable. The variance is computed through chance distribution and inverse chance distribution"

Thus, the expectation of uncertain random variable is the mean of values of the uncertain variable or its computed value.

We assume in the following that E(uncertainty of R) can be taken for the dispersion of R or V(R) for simplification purposes.

If we assume that the expectation of Risk uncertainty is the variance of risk,

We find that the expression of the variance of risk is a polynomial of the expectation of risk with coefficients as functions of the parameters α and μ assumed since the definition of the structuring of risk.

This dynamic formulation is very common in Economics literature and is intended in finance to express dynamic financial phenomena.

In the financial economics literature, there is a consensus that there exists a positive relation between risk and return.

Nevertheless, the empirical findings so far have been contradictory.

These contradictions are the result of negative skew in the distribution of portfolio excess return and the fact that the estimation of intertemporal asset prices models are based on symmetric log likelihood specificities.

We begin with the basic definition of variance of risk assuming risk is a random variable.

$Var(r) = Exp((r)^2) - (Exp(r))^2$

And an extrapolation from the definition of Profitability Gap

Profitability Gap = Potential profitability – Actual profitability

= (Effectively likely risk)* (Measure of risk)

Assuming potential profitability is the remuneration of overall risk effectively likely risk is equal to (Risk – uncertainty).

As long as:

Risk = uncertainty + effectively likely risk (like in section 2)

Now the measure of risk is:

The cumulation of risk pertaining to credit activity, risk pertaining to excess volatility of stock markets and projects risk which is profitability gap.

Assuming μ is the risk return tradeoff coefficient which is not necessarily scalar

This leads to Profitability gap= (Risk- Uncertainty) * ((Risk premiuns-Risk of NPLs) +(Stock market index-principal component of SMI)+ μ Profitability gap)

Risk = Porf gap *(1/((Risk premiums-Risk of NPls)+ (Stock market index-principal component of SMI) +μ Prof gap)) + Risk Uncertainty

The expectation of profitability gap is a certain scalar α multiplied by the expectation of risk

The expectation of the multiplier for prof gap is 1/ (1+α*μ* Exp (Risk))

Exp (R)= Var (R) + α*Exp (R)/(1+α*μ*Exp(R))

Var (R) = E (R) - α*E (R)/(1+α*μ*E(R)) (0)

$Var (R) = E(R)^2 – (E(R))^2$ (1)

$E (R)^2 = Var (R) + (E(R))^2$

$= Var (R) + (Var (R) + αE (R)/(1+αμE(R)))^2$

$= Var (R) (1+ Var (R) +2 αE (R)/(1+αμE(R)) + α^2E^2 (R)/(1+αμE(R))^2$

Substituting into (1) gives

$Var (R) = Var (R) (1+ Var (R) +2 αE (R)/(1+αμE(R)) + α^2E^2 (R)/(1+αμE(R))^2 - E^2(R)$

$= Var (R) (1+ Var (R) +2 αE (R)/(1+αμE(R)) + α^2-1- α^2μ^2E^2(R)- 2 αμE(R)/(1+ α^2μ^2E^2(R)+ αμE(R)))$

Setting expressions of Var R on the left handside yields

$Var(R)* (1-1-Var (R)-2αE(R)/(1+αμE(R))=E^2(R)* (α^2-1- α^2μ^2E^2(R)- 2αμE(R)/(1+$

$\alpha^2\mu^2E^2(R)+ \alpha\mu E(R))$

$-Var^2(R)= 2Var (R) \alpha E(R)/ (1+\alpha\mu E(R)) + E^2(R)* (\alpha^2-1- \alpha^2\mu^2E^2(R)- 2\alpha\mu E(R)/(1+ \alpha^2\mu^2E^2(R) + \alpha\mu E(R))$

Therefore

$Var(R)= -2 \alpha E(R)/ (1+\alpha\mu E(R)) - E^2(R)/Var(R)* (\alpha^2-1- \alpha^2\mu^2E^2(R)- 2\alpha\mu E(R)/(1+ \alpha^2\mu^2E^2(R) + \alpha\mu E(R))$

$Var (R) = E (R) - \alpha E (R)/(1+\alpha\mu E(R))= E(R)(1- \alpha/(1+\alpha\mu E(R)))$

The second expression leads to

$E(R)(1- \alpha/(1+\alpha\mu E(R))) +2 \alpha E(R)/ (1+\alpha\mu E(R)) =- E^2(R)/Var(R)* (\alpha^2-1- \alpha^2\mu^2E^2(R)- 2\alpha\mu E(R)/(1+ \alpha^2\mu^2E^2(R)+ \alpha\mu E(R))$

Therefore

$E(R) (1+ \alpha/ (1+\alpha\mu E(R)) = - (E^2(R)/ (E(R)(1- \alpha/ (1+\alpha\mu E(R))) * (\alpha^2-1- \alpha^2\mu^2E^2(R)- 2\alpha\mu E(R))/(1+ \alpha^2\mu^2E^2(R)+ \alpha\mu E(R))$

Simplifying both sides by E(R) leads to

$1+ \alpha/ (1+\alpha\mu E(R)) = (1/(1- \alpha/ (1+\alpha\mu E(R))) * (\alpha^2-1- \alpha^2\mu^2E^2(R)- 2\alpha\mu E(R))/(1+ \alpha^2\mu^2E^2(R)+ \alpha\mu E(R))$

Now we make use of the notion of implicit differentiation with respect to E(R) both sides

The first term in the right hand side is denoted by f and the second term by g

The development of the implicit differenciation leads to

$- \alpha^2\mu/(1+\alpha\mu E(R))^2= f'g-fg'$ with respect to E(R)

$- \alpha^2\mu/(1+\alpha\mu E(R))^2 = (1/Var^2(R))* (2 \alpha^2\mu^2E(R) +2\alpha\mu)(1+ \alpha\mu E(R)- \alpha) (1+ \alpha^2\mu^2E^2(R)+2 \alpha\mu E(R))-(1- \alpha+ \alpha^2\mu^2E^2(R)+2 \alpha\mu E(R))((\alpha^2\mu+ \alpha\mu E(R)+(1+ \alpha\mu E(R)- \alpha)(2 \alpha^2\mu^2E^2(R)+ \alpha\mu))/ (1+ \alpha\mu E(R))$

with introducting equation (0), Var(R) = E(R) – E(R)/(1+αμE(R)) to the right hand side and substituting by Var(R)

We take $Var^2(R)$ to the numerator of the left handside and we develop the right hand side for E(R) then we replace Var(R) by y and E(R) by x

We find

$Y^2 = 1/(\alpha^2\mu x)*(x^4(2\alpha^5\mu^5 + 2\alpha^4\mu^4 - 2\alpha^4\mu^4(2-\alpha)) + x^3(2\alpha^4\mu^4(1-\alpha\mu) - 2\alpha^4\mu^4 + 2\alpha^3\mu^3) + x^2(2\alpha^3\mu^2(1-\alpha\mu) - 2\alpha^3\mu^3 - 2\alpha^3\mu^3(2-\alpha) - 2\alpha^2\mu^3(\alpha^2-\alpha) + \alpha^2\mu^2(1+2\alpha\mu)) + x(-4\alpha\mu^2(\alpha^2-\alpha) + \alpha\mu(1+2\alpha\mu)) + 2\alpha\mu(1-\alpha) - 2\mu(\alpha^2-\alpha)$.

By using implicit differenciation once again with respect to x we find

$d(y^2/dx) = 2\, d(y/x)\, y$

$d(y/x) = -2x$ because $Var(R) = E(R^2) - E^2(R)$ hence $dVar(R)/dE(R) = -2E(R)$ as $dE^2(R)/d(E(R) = 0$

assuming $E(R^2)$ is independent of E(R)

hence $-4xy = 1/(8\alpha^2\mu x^2)*(x^4 A + x^3 B + x^2 C + xD + E) - 1/(4\alpha^2\mu x^2)*(x^3 4A + x^2 3B + x\, 3C + D)$

Therefore simplifying the above equation gives a polynomial function of fixed coefficients with respect to E(R) and various powers.

Hence, We have shown by a mathematical proof that the variance of risk is a polynomial function of the expectation of risk

This proof displays the merit to show that following this structure of risk like adopted under the purview of our structuring, realistic concerns about dynamic structure of risk are highlighted and theoretical assertions pervasive in the literature about the polynomial structure of dynamic complex systems like the risk structure and composition are verified.

Yu and Loskot (2022) stated that: " Polynomial distributions provide a superior flexibility over other canonical distributions, albeit at a cost of large number of parameters and the support interval is constrained to a finite range of values. The main advantage of polynomial distributions is that they can yield parameterized closed form mathematical expressions as well as offer a much greater flexibility in modeling time evolution of probability distribution for example when describing causal interactions in complex systems and modeling state transitions in dynamic systems"

The concise fathoming of risk distribution helps proceed to comprehensive early warning for the sake of making risk management serve for financial instability mitigation and ensure better resilience from the onslaught of financial meltdowns under the scope of better shaped prudential surveillance schemes.

This is due to the fact that once risk distribution over time based on time series data is better framed the issue of early warning gets more stringent and the likelihood of forecasting future evolution of risk gets better ensured which allows better forecasting of coming resilience from financial instability and better financial sectors' supervision in terms of systemic exposure.

The time series expression of Risk should be a PDL polynomial distributed lag which corresponds to an ARDL autoregressive distributed lags model but for whome variance is not constant but polynomial as the variance is expressed as a polynomial in function of expectation.

It is worthless to state that financial phenomena should be modeled accurately in order to pave the way for an accurate estimation for forecasting purposes and hence either early warning modeling or merely displaying new features in the Balance scorecard for monitoring and policy making.

Most microfinancial phenomena are odeled ARDL or VAR or seasonal models.

But the accurate estimation technique that conveys most of specification for Risk is the PDL or polynomial distributed lags estimation technique.

As long as the risk distribution is polynomial which is tributary to the imperfection imbedded in credit market that are structured either in cartel or monopolistic competition with the implicit agreements among banks on risk premiums that bound the loan prices and the imperfect competition on similar products.

From imperfect competition that distinguishes the credit market and according to the second dividends theory it is obvious that the argument according to which prudential restrictions although beneficial introduce frictions is pointless.

Indeed according to the second dividend theory summing up imperfections comes out with lesser distortionnary market

Hence the primary feasability of introducing prudential restrictions is due essentially to the fact that the credit sector is already imperfect otherwise the whole apparatus of prudential surveillance would have been rejected as a key solution to mitigate financial instability that is bound paramountly to distortions in the credit market.

Hence the rationale for recoursing to frictions as prudential instruments claimed to tackle the issue of exposureto financial instability is the fact that the credit sector already is exposed to imperfections which renders additional exposureto distortions partially offsetting the initial imperfections due to the market structure of the credit market.

3. THE BASEL FRAMEWORKS WEAKNESSES AND THE REQUIREMENT TO UNVEIL ITS SHORTCOMINGS

3.1 THE BASEL FRAMEWORKS' WEAKNESSES

According to Borio and Crockett (2000), one of the vulnerabilities of the Basel II and III instruments mentioned in the literature is that the cyclical and structural dimensions are predominant, generating opacity, interconnectivity and complexity that get in the way of good prudential supervision.

The main instruments frequently used are:

Reserve requirements (RR), Loan-to-deposit ratio. (LTD), Counter-cyclical capital buffers (CCB), Internal Capital Adequacy Pricing (ICAAP), Interest rate risk in banking risk (RTIRB).m Loan-to-value ratio (LTV)

These instruments are taking the functional form of ratios which does not give precedence to economic concepts with concise analytical merits, such as the marginal effects analyses included in the (sensitivities).

The Instruments used would be static rather than dynamic in terms of dependence on the time factor.

The Functional Form undermines the merits of considering marginal impact effects with overriding implications for economic policy and economic analysis.

The instruments are shown to be unsuitable for short-term equilibrium cyclical adjustments (with the exception of counter-cyclical capital buffers) or long-term equilibrium longitudinal adjustments.

The relationships between financial stability and prudential instruments are implicit, and not materialized by concise quantitative estimates, but rather by PROBIT-type qualitative response models, which would be too non-contributory.

The main drawback of the Basel IV framework which is the so called revised standardized approach is that usually instruments are taking the form of probabilities (Risk measures) which are of low value (inferior to 1)

Figure 1: The revised standardized approach of Basel IV

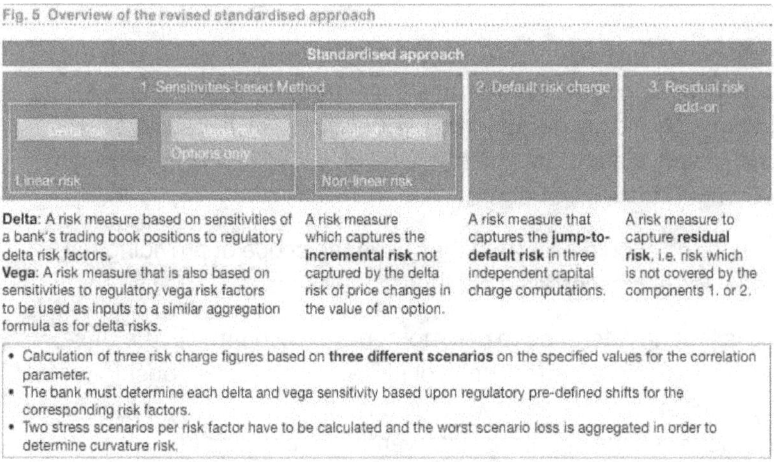

Source: The Basel Framework

The first critic to assert about this conventional framework is that, empirically, these correlation parameters are extracted from estimations of elasticities of the kind in Genc (2012) where there are four possibilities for formulations of elasticities each with a certain adequacy and goodness of fit depending on the value of the elasticity per se.

Eventually, with computations of sensitivities there would have been no problems. But still a main hindrance to the computation of the sensitivity is the specificity of the mathematical formula that requires having discrete functions that are derivable in mathematical analysis. If not estimation of the elasticity or computation of the economic simplification assumption is required.

The authors as documented in Banks and Al (1997) find that for values of sensitivities that are low it is that the approximation of the sensitivity ; the one that is commonly used in economics which is $e(A/B) = (\Delta A/\Delta B*B/A)$ performs better than any estimator corresponding to their estimation technique and to any oter estimation technique like the ECM (Error correction modeling) or ARDL (Autoregressive dynamic lags) by Perasan and Shin (2001).

Hence, due to the fact that it still stands approximate it is not a very concise estimator of the market risk which is the Basel IV sensitivity based instrument of the standardized approach based on sensitivities of market risk either linear or non-linear.

One main additional drawback or the second critic to be asserted is that the risk measures are not balanced in their formulations meaning that a sensitivity in numeric differs widely from a default risk computation which creates a mismatch in descriptive statistics and might result in neglecting the effect of sensitivities computations in variation.

A sum of three items should ascertain they have the scope of providing the same functional form to ascertain a balance in their scope.

The last critic is that no reference to risk moments is accounted in the Basel framework even though their effect on evolution of risk either ex-post for actual risk assessment or ex-ante for early warning assessment reveals of rudimental importance to better shape prudential intervention or supervision.

3.2 THE REQUIREMENT OF UNVEILING BASEL FRAMEWORK SHORTCOMINGS

It is obviously pre-required in terms of resilience from the onslaught of financial crises to tackle the root items lying behind financial instability in each sector.

Therefore, it is seemingly inaccurate to base resilience from financial instability on the Basel framework whose aim is specific to mitigating financial instability that affects the credit sector.

As a matter of fact, although financial instability pertaining to the credit sector is of commensurate importance and relevance, it still stands that a lot has to be achieved in terms of resilience from Stock market risk or financial instability coming from excess volatility of share prices as they might herald the onslaught of a Stock market crush for whom an adequate and specific prudential surveillance framework should be engineered and adopted for the sake of avoiding financial vulnerability that comes from excess volatility of share prices and might be exacerbated by a Stock crush or excess bullish slope of the stock index that might be due to excessive speculation.

Excessive speculation is in many instance is abrupt meaning it might erupt unexpectedly and in other cases it is predictable by the cross correlation of share prices that present a comparable pattern of evolution and might move in parralell which is a signal of a vulnerability that requires more scrutiny and to be covered in a section that will flow.

As far as the use of ratios that are seemingly neglecting key features of economic functions allowing for structural and conjectural analyses and marginal effects calibration, there still stands that a PhD dissertation presented in (2022) by M Miras Marzouki still unpublished that discussed complementary instruments to Basel II and III framework and that used a sensitivity approach based on a macroeconomic perspective which presumably performs better in terms of estimation with high values of sensitivities that according to Banks (1997) provide estimators with more accuracy than the approximation commonly used in economics that would be a must as an estimator for the Basel IV standardized approach.

For this estimations the PhD dissertation entitled : « A theory of financial strategic foresight and prudential engineering : Case of Tunisia » used the estimation method ARDL autoregressive dynamic lags for time series regressions and BOUND tests for long run early warning systems.

As far as the qualification of financial stability is concerned, it should be pointed out that this is a phenomenon that can be qualified rather than quantified, and which consequently requires qualifiers aimed at determining it, or phenomena closely related to it such as (MP efficiency, banking system efficiency, borrower solvency, crowding-out effect, etc.) rather than effects as enshrined in conventional instruments (capital buffers, reserve requirements, liquidity risk ratios, etc.).

The sensitivities to be proposed can be interpreted as phenomena, whereas the conventional Bale ratios are effects, which would be ill-suited to qualify a non-quantifiable phenomenon such as financial stability, if not by a qualitative response model of the PROBIT type, with two alternatives - one to confirm stability and one to deny it - which would be insufficient to qualify financial instability Basel IV framework is based on a sensitivity approach with a methodology based on market risk assessment extracted what is called uncertainty microeconomics.

In definitive, as much as this subject is concerned there is a lot of skepticism concerning functional forms and theoretical meanings of adopted prudential instruments that raises a debate on effectuality of making accurate use of them when dealing with resilience from onslaught of financial meltdowns.

Still it stands that overall these are meant to exclusively deal with systemic exposure that emanates from the banking sector whereas prudential surveillance is meant for mitigation of financial instability root items.

Those are not necessarily originating from the banking sector but can eventually occur in the Stock market sector due to excess volatility of share prices that can exacerbate market risk far beyond tolerable to ensure stability of the financial system or what can emulate from the risk of onslaught of Stock market crashes eventually whose probability of occurrence increases with excess volatility of Stock share prices.

Therefore, a lot of criticism should be conveyed to the Basel framework in general and there is a lot of doubt as to whether it is an effectual prudential framework that can ensure effective resilience of financial stability and mitigate systemic risk to the financial system.

An issue of prominent relevance for the subject matter is about investor risk appetite for whom a lot of concern should expressed as to whether it is pro-cyclical with the business cycle counter-cyclical or a-cyclical because business cycle effects play a predominant role in terms of the effect of economic performance on financial stability at a first place and as long as monetary policy is intended primarily for price and output stability there is much concern about the effect of business cycle fluctuations on the interaction between prudential policy and monetary policy.

3.3 RISK MITIGATION AND VARIANCE OF RISK ATTENUATION

Among the main shortcomings of the Basel frameworks stands the fact that its scope is exclusively to mitigate risk.

But there should be room for consideration of variance of risk assessments and framing as risk is a random variable and the more it is dispersed in probability of occurrence the more it is unpredictable hence not subject to accurate consideration and not accounted for in a precise way.

Thus a more appropriate goal for prudential surveillance should be risk variance framing alongside mitigation of expectation of risk as currently adopted and also it should consider targeting forecasting of future evolution of skew and kurtosis of risk tails as they reveal of rudimental relevance for the assessment of future evolution of risk.

Alongside risk mitigation of risk coming from liquidity and credit risk from the banking perspective and excess volatility and hedging deteriorating consequences coming from trading of securities, it is clear that a perspective directed towards economic and business projects where project risk is divided into equity relative risk and external borrowing relative risk grasps the credit risk pertaining to the banking sector and one part of volatility in the share prices coming from disinformativeness with respect to share prices and profitability outcomes pertaining to the stock market sector.

As long as project risk should be conveyed more impetus adequate concern should be directed towards variance of risk as mainly expectations have dispersed probabilities depending on what performance really occurs.

Hence it matters a lot how would realizations of earnings happen to be per se and compared to each other.

Project risk should be considered rather from the perspective of variance of risk rather than risk in itself.

In this respect the variance of risk matters far more than its expectation provided risk is taken for a random variable.

3.4 THE NEED FOR BACKTESTING AND A GENERAL APPRAISAL OF THE BASEL FRAMEWORK SHORTCOMINGS

Acerbi and Szchely (2015) stated that:

"Backtesting is a test used to ensure that the model yields forecasts that are in line with the actual realities in other words it is used to check the validity and viability of the model in capturing risk".

This misconception of backtesting has become the root obstacle for the Basel committee to fully implement Expected shortfall as the standard regulatory risk measure. Indeed, they found out that"ES cannot be used to rank different point forecasts in a decision theoretically way" as stated in Ziegel (2014).

Summing up the above-mentioned analyses about the standard regulatory frameworks methodological approaches of risk capturing and prudential instruments setting in Basel II and III agreements, it is obvious that these regulatory frameworks should be subjected to partial reconsideration and up grading if not full reconsideration with an ulterior engineering methodology of newly set instruments paving the way for a full grasping of the pre-requirements for an adequate implementation of the must of risk mitigation and financial vulnerability attenuation as purported by the Basel committee but through an other perspective of instruments setting and modeling.

The attempt made by the Basel IV framework about upgrading the expected shortfall about market risk has displayed many advantages drawing the wedge between the requirements of backtesting various point estimates through the mention of the key features of risk suggestible to three scenarios.

The three risk charge figures which are namely the Delta Vega and the incremental risk require an extrapolation based on three different scenarios on the specified values for the correlation parameter.

These key risk factors are the key contribution of Basel IV and still represent a shortage in terms of complexity, interconnectiveness and opacity like stated by Borio and Crockett (2000)

Besides and most obviously there is an urgent call of complementing the entire prudential framework aimed at insulating the credit market from market risk summarised in credit and liquidity risk in brief to deal with a market risk emanating from an other financial sector.

These are under the purview of the scope of Stock market prudential engineering presented and discussed later in the paper in Section 4.

3.5 EARLY WARNING AS A PREREQUISITE FOR UNVEILING FUTURE THREATS TO FINANCIAL STABILITY

Early warning in prudential surveillance is assumed to prompt forward guidance of key time dependent and financial instability related items in a way that dismays future exposure to financial meltdowns. Prudential as instruments as for Basel II and III and even those sensitivity based of Basel IV are bound to shortsightedness in that they target the short run. They do not display features that shields for expected futures exposure to financial meltdowns or sources of systemic exposure.

According to us there should be room for conducting co-integration or Bound tests for variables that are not stationary of the same order like in Perasan and Shin (2001) for Delta, Vega and the residual risk and the default risk at least if not as a minimum requirement to be conditional on further analyses such as Markov switching modeling and related jump effects tracing for Basel IV framework of additional instruments.

The Bound test should test for the long run relationship with a benchmark risk sensitivity which is the willingness of the banking system to bear excessive risk for the search for yield motivation which is the sensitivity of new production of credit to the private sector to money market rate or e(NCPS/MMR).

Henceforth with an implicit testing for co-integration or Bound testing, we ensure that early warning is available in that the prudential regulator is alarmed in advance from future threats whenever over the long run the various types of risk ; Delta, Vega and the residual risk for market risk have long run relationships with the benchmark risk that expresses the Imprudence of the banking sector in terms of risk exposure for a search for yield motivation.

The rationale for the chosen benchmark for excessive risk is that private credit bears excessive risk exposure and is beneficial in terms of profitability for banks.

Yet the reasoning that early warning should prevail is also valid for upgrading Basel II and III as even this framework is shortsighted in that it does not proceed to early warning for the sake of ensuring resilience from the onslaught of financial meltdowns stemming from financial instability with early warning or in advance what requires adopting long run relationship testing as available in co-integration and Bound testing.

4. THE BALANCED SCORECARD RISK RELATED INSTRUMENT AND ITS IMPLICATION ON THE INTEGRATION OF FINANCIAL SECTORS

The Balanced Score Card is a key concept for the integration of financial sectors.

According to Abdali (2013) « The integration between performance and risk management enables organizations to both monitor and evaluate the performance effectually through the balanced scorecard and to prevent further unfavorable consequences resulting from uncertain performance ».

Gordona, Loeba and Tseng (2009) discussed the new trend in viewing the risk management. They noticed the new trend of holistic view of risk management which is commonly referred to as enterprise risk management (ERM).

According to them : « Five factors have an impact on the ERM. These factors are ; the environmental uncertainty, the industry competition, the firm complexity, and its size and the Board of directors' monitoring »

These factors fall into the scope of rational assessment of investment by traders in the secondary market.

Their assessment is intended to depict expected beneficial investment opportunities and does affect fluctuations of the Stock market index with pikes and troughs.

But, as far as financial stability pertaining to the stock market is concerned, it still stands that the key factor or criterion of prominent relevance for excess volatility of the Stock market index which is compromising for financial stability is the cross correlation between share prices which is not available in the BSC. Nonetheless the BSC can provide a clue about the patterns of the Stock market index and henceforth through the diversification of trading for the sake of disentangling the traders from the commonly followed behavior that binds the average trend of the stock index.

This has the effect of dampening excess volatility up to a certain limit.

Bu it is yet uncertain how far does the portfolio diversification of rational investors affect excess fluctuations and how far it affects excess volatility.

Anyway the BSC is expected to provide a clear assessment of expected risk and uncertainty about future corporations performance financially and non financially.

As far as the BSC is concerned Beasley, Chen Nunez and Wright (2006) put an emphasis on the potential benefits of developing a set key risk indicator KRI.

They stated that : « The potential value of KRI may be derived from different contributions such as risk appetite by determining an appropriate threshold for action at different organizations levels. Risk and opportunity identified by designing KRIs to alert management to trends that may affect the achievement of organizational objectives or may introduce new opportunities. Risk treatment by serving mechanisms for organizational units and Risk reporting by providing measurable data conclusive to aggregation »

These features fall into the scope of annihilating the cross correlation among share prices as they display for the trader the required tools to diversify his trading strategy so that it gets disentangled from mass comparable trading strategies that not only motivate cross correlations among share prices but also minimize expected earnings as they are shared opportunities rather than innovations in depicting favorable opportunities most expected to be beneficial.

The BSC draws a wedge between unveiling the risk management root items and hence the creditworthiness of the corporation into consideration and its effect or contribution in credit risk or risk of non-performing loans for the credit sector which is a building block of financial instability from the standpoint of the credit sector and the rational information gathering sources for traders in the Stock market that involves efficiency and stability whereby as stated earlier efficiency of the stock market is related to its stability.

Nevertheless it still stands that financial stability ffrom the stock market perspective is compromised by excess volatility of stock prices whose fluctuations are essentially due to cross correlated stocks i.e stocks that vary in the same direction once a perturbation occurs.

Besides basically financial stability from the stock market standpoint is threatened by irrationally based trading or trading that is more likely to be beneficial and lead to a bandwagon effect of following up or what we might call a speculative attack that compromises tremendously stock market stability.

The balanced scorecard affects considerably the MBV and by of consequence Stock market efficiency.

It is also obvious that it affects excess volatility of share prices even if there are claims that investor trading patterns are driven by sentiment and irrationally cast patterns of purchasing and selling of Stock.

The BSC ensures that an adequate assessment of risk aspects pertaining to corporations can exhibit future patterns of profitability and by a way of consequence make information accessible to traders more adequate and less asymmetric fact that ensures least volatility in face of clear foresightedness of future profitability expectations.

Thus affordability of a reliable balanced scorecard in itself can help mitigate financial instability provided the irrationality of traders is rational up to a certain point which is not guaranteed.

As a matter of fact, disrespectfully of the fact that the risk assessment of an entrepreneurial activity of a quoted corporation is trivial for financial stability pertaining to the Stock market sector it still stands of commensurate relevance for financial stability considerations pertaining to the credit sector.

Indeed, borrowers' credit worthiness and credit scoring which are of prominent relevance for credit risk assessed by banks, the BSC provides key information of prominent relevance for unveiling uncertainty for risk assessment by the credit sector.

By a way of consequence the assessment of borrowers' credit worthiness becomes more accurate and credit risk which is proportional to financial instability is attenuated.

The interaction between the stock market sector and the credit sector is better fathomed once we settle an accurate and precise BSC.

This is essentially due to the fact that rational assessment of corporations by traders in the stock market goes in parallel with the corporations solvency and its credit worthiness vis-à-vis the bank or the loan supplier which affects financial instability of the credit sector and eventually borrowing costs subject to risk premiums assessments.

Excess volatility of stock prices results from cross correlations between stock prices fluctuations and not excess risk entailed by the corporations operations.

As long as risk is taken into consideration especially if it is clearly specified In the balance scorecard investor trading behavior becomes rational subject to objective assessment.

By a way of consequence earnings prospects are attenuated considerably except for those investment opportunities that surprise the market.

Indeed these beneficial trading opportunities cannot be involving the concern of rationally guided investors that analyze objectively their investment opportunities based on available information including the balance scorecard.

Nevertheless it still stands that the better shaped is the BSC the closer is the MBV (market to book value) to 1 and the more efficient is the stock market.

5. EARLY WARNING SYSTEMS, LONG RUN PRUDENTIAL SURVEILLANCE CONVERGENCE AND MARKOV SWITCHING REGIMES

The process is as follows:

Ensuring a stable income stream ias a priority for banks maintains resilience from the onslaught of liquidity risk that triggers credit risk.

Indeed, as continuous profitability decreases liquidity behaves as well. This drives the bank motivated by the search for yield motivation to incurring more risk because risky assets bear more risk premiums that increase profitability and this exacerbates financial instability.

A rule of thumb in financial management consists in ensuring stable future income streams to diminish future liquidity or turnover risk.

Therefore maintaining continuous stable income streams through ensuring a ceiling on long term debt dissuades the bank in advance to incur the hindrance of supporting a risk return tradeoff later in what we call an early warning procedure to avoid future vulnerability and foresightedness about stable income streams.

Early warning in the stock market occurs by smoothing the super-multiplier effect. This can be eased through inciting long term placement either by following the Board of Governors of the Federal Reserve System (2023) that call the urge for ensuring long term debt obviously through decreasing the cost of long term debt and thus increasing the cost of long term equity financing which occurs through the financial accelerator effect or through adding favorable extra conditions for long term stakeholders through allowing them for benefiting from more governance and bargaining power on corporations management policy.

The effect would be decreased share price volatility over the long run and henceforth mitigated financial instability.

Smoothing the super-multiplier effect requires capping the long term borrowing rate and in parallel ceiling the long term placement dividend rate So that share prices volatility is decreased in synchrony with ensured long run income streams for the credit sector.

And hence stability of both financial sectors is ensured

5.1 CURRENTLY ADOPTED EARLY WARNING SYSTEMS

In parallel to early warning measures, federal agencies have provided lately supervision requirement for large banks to maintain long term debt to ensure resilience from losses and financial stability as stated by the Board of Governors of the Federal Reserve System (2023).

Figure 2: Approaches to supervisory Risk and arly warning systems

Table 2: Approaches to supervisory risk assessment and early warning systems – generic features

	Assessment of current financial condition	Forecasting future financial condition	Use of quantitative analysis and statistical procedures	Inclusion of qualitative assessments	Specific focus on risk categories	Link with formal supervisory action
Supervisory ratings - on-site - off-site	*** ***	* *	* **	*** **	* **	*** *
Financial ratio and peer group analysis	***	*	***	*	**	*
Comprehensive bank risk assessment systems	***	**	**	**	***	***
Statistical models	**	***	***	*	**	*

*   not significant
**   significant
***   very significant

Souce: Early warning Systems

These approaches fall under the scope of foresightedness and early warning as mainly most prudential measures of Basel II, III and IV target the short run and are intended to mitigate financial instability over the short run.

We will focus on the three columns; forecasting future financial conditions, the use of quantitative analysis and statistical procedures as well as the inclusion of qualitative assessments.

Indeed, in the referred to literature as stated in Sahajwala and Bergh (2000) there are three main types of early warning systems:

-Scoring models of credit rating and awareness notation in instance

- Qualitative response models of the type logit with two outcomes. This type of early warning models although relying on strong theoretical assumptions lacks contribution in terms of interpretation of endogenous variables as they have two outcomes of the type pass or fail

-Artificial intelligence models currently used by several prudential authorities of the G10 countries

We propose with reference to the sensitivity based modeling discussed above a quantitative response models whereby the sensitivity expressing an impact effect is regressed in a time series regression for forecasting purposes. Once it is interpreted the values of the sensitivity explained provide a vast array of likely solutions to be interpreted accordingly to its interpretation.

This method clearly outperforms the two first methods although Artificial intelligence models are claimed to be very effectual but they remain essentially not statistical in nature or based on quantitative econometric analysis and forecasting which might be troublesome in terms of economic and financial interpretation.

For such contributive value the notion of sensitivity is a clue that annihilates disinformation about the quality of future key variables in that it displays the main feature through its merits of qualifying impact effects to show in quantitative response models qualitative information.

For example the sensitivity of new credit supply to the private sector to the money market rate is measurable as a quantitative variable and qualifies at the same time the notion of willingness of the banking system to bear excessive risk disrespectfully of the fact that it provides information on whether indeed the banking system would be willing to bear excessive risk or not.

Sensitivities should be modeled for the sake of setting early warning systems taking everything else equal about the method adopted for long run correlation or forecasting or whether Artificial intelligence should be adopted or not.

Besides for early warning purposes a deep concern should be directed toward fathoming risk distribution and moments in order to permit to draw a certain pattern of future evolution of dispersion probability of risk expectation and to have better shaped clues about skew and Kurtosis that show where distribution is biased in the present and future if time series are adopted.

The accurate fathoming of risk distribution permits to forecast in advance the interval of risk dispersion provided it is subjected to adjustment with respect to the variable items that are encompassed in its expression the uncertainty item the business cycle related item and the stable item.

5.2 CONVERGENCE AND GRAVITY: AN APPRAISAL OF DYNAMIC CONTAGION ASSESSMENT

The concept of convergence involves the notion of catch up between financial development levels which is driven by the process of gravity across financial systems' development.

The difference between gravity and convergence is that convergence is dynamic gravity which is assessed statistically across weighing of various point in time determinants and evolves to convergence when we add up the time dimension targeting the long run.

The scope of convergence is an assessment of early warning about contagion.

The law of gravitation stipulates that catch up celerity is inversely proportional to the financial stability discrepancies

For high discrepancies of levels of financial development catch up is fast.

The convergence is a process that is intricating because it assumes the prévalence of two effects that Work simultaneously contrariwise among levels of financial development and financial stability levels in a region.

So either way catch up effect works through convergence between levels of financial development or levels of financial stability.

When the discrepancies between financial stability levels are high convergence works through this channel and indeed discrepancies between financial system levels is low.

When financial stability levels are close financial development are far away and convergence works through catch up of levels of development.

The scenario of selfsustaining convergence is least likely indeed because there are two simultaneous processes that work in same time.

The total effect of convergence is the sum of the gravitation effect and attraction effect.

The attraction occurs because of discrepancies in financial system effectiveness levels whereas the gravitation occurs because of discrepancies in financial stability levels.

If the first effect outweights the second the final effect is convergence.

If the second effect outweights the effect is gravitation or less convergence.

Contagion here works as an accelerator of convergence because it takes financial stability closer and hence financial efficacy farther away and by a way of consequence convergence faster.

By measuring accurately convergence of financial sectors financial instability through gravity index we can fathom the pattern of evolution of cross correlation between financial sectors likelihood of contagion through time.

Hence contagion or propagation detection can be informative in terms one point in time propagation likelihood whereas convergence through gravity can be informative about how does this propagation likelihood evolve through time and can provide tool for deploying early warning graspung the long run pattern of propagation of financial crises in one region.

Hence contagion detection is a descriptive instrument of awareness whereas convergence is an analytical instrument of awareness.

Eventually the overall pattern of evolution of convergence can be countered by institutional adjustments insulating one local financial system from risk of contagion from overseas financial systems.

Thought convergence concerns financial deepening it is obvious that as documented in the literature financial efficiency is positively correlated with financial deepening and as long as financial efficiency is inversely related to financial stability, the argument of convergence still holds in the opposite direction for financial instability considerations.

Indeed as financial development path converge to each other for instance à financial certain level of country A convergence to a financial deepening level of country B it is obvious that financial stability of country A convergence to financial instability of country B where financial deepening is an indicator of efficiency of the financial system.

By a way of consequence we can proxy the convergence index of financial deepening by the convergence index of financial instability or the inverse of the index for financial stability.

$E=MC^2$ proxied from the Einstein law of energy

CONVERGENCE IS THE ENERGY OF GRAVITATION MEANING THAT

$CONVERGENCE_{ij}$=(FINANCIALDEVELOPMENT$_i$-FINANCIAL DEVELOPMENT$_j$)*$GRAVITY_{ij}^2$

$GRAVITY_{ij}$=FINANCIAL DEVELOPMENT$_i$*FINANCIAL DEEVELOPMENT$_j$/(FINANCIAL OPENESSi-FINANCIAL OPENESS$_j$)2

$CONVERGENCE_{ij}$=(FINANCIAL DEVELOPMENTi-FINANCIAL DEVELOPMENTj)* FINANCIAL $DEVELOPMENT_i^2$*FINANCIAL $DEVELOPMENT_j^2$/ (FINANCIAL OPENESSi-FINANCIAL OPENESSj)4

The prominent feature of this index is that it provides insights on the long run pattern of evolution of predisposition to incur cross country contagion.

Hence, the convergence computation provides an upgraded prudential instrument providing a better assessment than the conventional contafgion assessment risk. This instrument falls intothe scope of early warning from likely risks in the long run. Here risks are quantitative as well as qualitative.

5.3 MARKOV SWITCHING REGIMES FOR JUMP EFFECTS

One main feature of key salient instruments is that they are subject to a Brownian motion process or a jump process like credit risk as stated in Tak Kuen Siu (2010) where he discussed a Markov Regime Switching Marked Point Process for short rate analysis with credit risk where he emphasized that it is of commensurate importance to take into account jumping processes such as Markov switching regime processes because their adverse implications herald unexpectedly.

Therefore, as long as we discuss early warning, alongside the conventional time varying long run relationship as imbedded in co-integration and Bound tests, there should be room for testing for Markov switching regimes or brownian processes to be forwarded guided with respect to jump effects that herald unexpectedly for Markovian switching regimes and Brownian motions that are probabilistic and statistical phenomena with continuous innovations through time.

According to Tak Kuen Siu (2010) « Some information items such as surprise information and extraordinary market events may have large economic impact on short rates and cause jumps ».

He reiterated that: « Short rate models based on Brownian information flows may not be appropriate to describe large movements. Jump diffusion processes or related processes incorporate large jumps such as Markov switching regimes »

Thus, it is obvious that the kind of Markov switching regimes for credit risk or liquidity risk or rather illiquidity risk are not forecast able by conventional short run instruments toolkits that are especially targeting financial instability mitigation for the sake of abiding contingencies of the onslaught of financial meltdowns that might erupt abruptly and unexpectedly.

5.4 THE REQUIREMENT OF BACKTESTING

The most important item in early warning is back-testing which is a type of retro diction and cross validation applied to previous time periods.

This procedure aims at drawing patterns for risk items that overlap and reproduce in order to better shape early warning.

Modeling should be quantitative to provide concise parameters and phase shifts more likely than qualitative log-odds to frame the interval of evolution of predictions of risk and its moments.

Even risk moments should be subjected to back-testing because probability distribution shows likelihood in a certain time point whereas back-testing them might show a pattern of reproduction not depictable through probability distribution.

6. -EFFECTS OF INFORMATION ASSYMETRIES AND COST OF AGENCY ON STOCK PRICES VOLATILITY

The effects of agency costs and information asymmetries such as free riding and moral hazard are transmitted to bank profitability through the credit risk channel.

The effects of leverage and the super-multiplier amplify uncertainty about risk rating and ultimately affect banking efficiency and private investment.

Credit scoring and the assessment of borrowers' creditworthiness are subject to asymmetries, which significantly affect credit production and hence bank profitability, since most asset profitability is derived from credit production.

The more agency costs and information asymmetries prevail, the more bank profitability is deteriorated through unrecovered credits.

Thus there is a negative relationship between agency costs and information asymmetries and bank profitability.

In order to stop the circumvention of prudential measures of banking supervision, bank profitability should increase to dissuade bank management from resorting to malicious practices such as retargeting of bank customers and unfairness such as setting higher risk premiums for households than for firms in order to generate excess profit margins and to persuade shareholders to introduce more equity capital in order to favor the reduction of liquidity risk and to be able to generate excess profits by bearing a higher credit risk.

In order to increase ex-ante bank profitability, arrangement costs and information asymmetries would have to be reduced, and for this banks would have to rely less on the client histories provided by the scoring agencies and carry out more rigorous, albeit more costly, feasibility studies of projects.

This is in order to reduce the costs of arrangement by learning effect and to reduce the information asymmetries by the reliability of the evaluation of the solvency of borrowers a priori and thus to be able to increase the banking profitability and to attenuate the systemic risk and the financial instability and perhaps even to attenuate the negative macroeconomic shocks such as well stated by the phenomenon of the super-multiplier according to which shocks perceived by the volatility of equity prices and therefore automatically of the profitability of assets are transmitted to the macroeconomic arena in an amplified manner.

Indeed, one can simultaneously act on the cost of agency and information asymmetries such as free riding, although this is contradictory.

In fact, by lowering the agency cost, one would think that banks would save on the collection and analysis of data on the creditworthiness of borrowers and credit ratings.

But it is necessary to say that by allocating a team specialized in the study of the feasibility of the projects, with the passing of time they acquire by phenomenon of learning of the aptitudes to well detect the profitable projects of those whose financing risks to reveal a not covered credit.

In this way, both the cost of development and free riding are considerably reduced.

6.1-IMPORTANCE OF EFFECTS OF BORROWERS CREDIT WORTHINESS ON STOCK MARKET STABILITY

As borrowers' credit worthiness improves external borrowing becomes less expensive there is a demand pull from stakeholders because of the financial acceleration corporations are better off Dividends decrease and share prices increase contrariwise to volatility which is dampened because of the bargaining power that is reduced for stakeholders and more bargaining power for corporations management which makes stability improve and stock market more resilient to the onslaught of financial distress like a stock market crash.

Contrariwise when borrowers' Creditworthiness deteriorates stock market sector is less stable in terms of financial stability.

6.2-IMPLICATIONS ON STABILITY AND PRUDENTIALITY

Borrowers credit worthiness affects tremendously the cost of external borrowing for corporations that are priced at the stock exchange.

An improvement in borrowers credit worthiness affects the leverage effect or the financial accelerator effect.

An improvement in the net worth of corporations is generally associated with an improvement in Borrowers credit worthiness which relaxes the cost of external borrowing in such a way that there exists a demand pull from corporations management with respect to equity thereby improving the bargaining power of the management with respect to stakeholders that react by decreasing fluctuations of the cost push on dividends.

The capital asset pricing model states that dividends are inversely proportional to share prices

This in turn makes fluctuations of share prices deteriorate.

Therefore an improvement in borrowers credit worthiness deteriorates excess volatility of share prices thereby exacerbationg stock market sector financial stability through the bargaining power channel whereby a lack of dependency on equity decreases volatility of dividends and by a way of consequence increases volatility of share prices deteriorating thereby the market risk in the stock market sector.

7. HEDGING RISK AND PRUDENTIALITY: AN APPRAISAL

It is considered that derivatives increase the efficiency of the financial system. Dy a way of consequence they deteriorate stability. I lere surges a conundrum whereby from one side derivatives hedge from losses and by a way of consequence market risk and from the other side by deteriorating stability they call the urge for further Prudential intervening. But as long as the most prominent role of prudential intervention is ensuring more stability. It is consented that prudential instruments are mainly purporting at mitigating the very source of market risk which is excess volatility.

But given the nature of hedging of derivatives, excess volatility does not necessarily compromise market risk for investors in the sense of presenting a source of loss.

So where does the threat from derivatives to stability really come from?

Corporate hedging affects directly Stock market stability through the risk management related issue affecting equity and henceforth valuation either book or market one and indirectly through its effect on the credit transmission mechanism of credit that by affecting monetary policy stance exerts an impact on overall financial stability and in special stock market stability.

The issue of prudential surveillance is especially concerned by the use of derivatives.

As a matter of fact; on the one hand by improving efficiency and stability the use of hedging instruments alleviate burdens on the task of prudential surveillance by making it easier to promote financial stability and efficiency; but on the other hand by helping create crises and increasing systemic risk in the case of speculation and speculative attacks on exchange positions the use of derivatives worsens the situation and urges the call for contagion targeting prudential instruments.

Hedging does play a macro prudential role by capping the riskiness of expected returns that are fundamental in increasing volatility of stock returns.

As a matter of fact volatility of stock returns is the core source of systemic risk in stock market as it is pro cyclical with its own industry average behavior of returns and the business cycle and determines the pattern of systemic exposure of the stock market because stock returns determine stock prices.

So by hedging we break the pattern of volatility and covariance between stock prices whenever hedging in itself is not systemic or does not hold for all similar stock securities.

Certainly hedging plays a macro prudential role but cannot be taken for a macro prudential instrument as it is not intended at mitigating financial vulnerability but at ensuring minimizing losses on returns.

As long as the objectives of hedging and prudential surveillance are different they cannot be taken for holding as fulfilling the same task.

A qualitative assessment of Risk is transmitted through financial sectors through hedging.

As long as hedging conveys a bias in the assessment of the MBV of coroporations, it follows that it generates a tradeoff between Risk in the credit sector and risk in the Stockmarket sector. Indeed, Shielding the Stock market from quantitative Risk of losses will exacerbate the qualitative exposure of the banking sector prominently.

Hedging is about a financial stategy of derivatives that derives from conventional financial instruments that uses financial instruments or market strategies to offset the risk of any adverse price movements.

Investors hedge one investment by making a trade in another.

In pure economic terms this introduces frictions that display merits in terms of expectations and probabilities of earnings for investors as it works as a warranty for shielding from losses.

But these frictions will essentially lead through contagion to a bad quality of assets whereby corporations hedging for the outcome of acquisitions and transactions that are quoted in the stock market are likely not to care about a criterion that affects tremendously the cost of borrowing which is the analogous source of financing for equity.

Henceforth this will introduce of bias of selection and exacerbate the financial stability of the credit market.

Indeed as long as the corporation assets are hedged against future losses i twill matter least for the corporation management if the cost of external borrowing is minimized. This will affect negatively borrowers' credit worthiness as the corporation management will no longer care about the way the financial intermediary which is the bank will shed the light on their probability of default or what could be called their borrowers 'credit worthiness this will introduce an information asymmetry which is adverse selection and will lead the corporation to have a misconduct about expansion projects appraisal and risk of default which will exacerbate financial stability from the credit sector side

The pervasiveness of information draws a wedge between stock market valuation and assets quality.

Usually stock that performs well is backed by a good quality assets which informs on a sound management of the corporation from which the asset derives from

This means that stock that performs well enough and that does not need hedging is that which corresponds to a sound management and therefore a fairly good borrowers credit worthiness.

The rule of thumb is that if the corporation does not default with the bank it is more likely to make its shares stand for a good asset and therefore perform well and not require hedging to ensure a benefit for investors.

So in definitive although hedging exerts a positive effect on Stock market financial stability it does exert a negative effect on credit market financial stability.

There is skepticism about its overall effect as it is tough to weigh the effect of warranting expected future losses in the stock market with the effect of a deterioration in borrowers' credit worthiness and the probability of default on loans which is very harmful in terms of financial stability.

8. GENERAL CONCLUSION

The fundamental added value of this research is about setting a new structure of formulation of Risk and the resulting distribution of risk that reveals complying to finance theoretical predilections of a polynomial structure.

Alongside key drawbacks of the currently adopted prudential fra;ework and the alternative solutions to annihilate its drawbacks the risk formulation dras the wedge of conventional framing of risk and one key issue which is early warning deployed either through sensitivity forecasting models with long run co-integration or jump effects models like the regime switching models.

There is an outstanding pervasiveness of prudential instruments displaying the major drawbacks of interconnectedness, complexity and opacity along with the inability of back-testing and other drawbacks such as inaccurate estimation ability of the risk charge figures Delta, Vega and the incremental risk for market risk pertaining to the credit sector as displayed in Basel IV and that should be dealt with accurately.

Financial vulnerability is more complex to mitigate in the framework related to the stock market because of the prevalence of excess volatility of stock as a key threat to Stock market stability and require engineering of the adequate instruments aiming at mitigating excess volatility of share prices.

Main features characterizing the credit market such as the prevalence of information asymmetries the relevance of taking into account borrowers' credit worthiness which are the corporations securitized in the stock exchange and the importance of Non-performing loans should be accounted for with deep concern whenever the financial accelerator effect and the super-multiplier effect are framed in perspective with the requirement of mitigating financial instability heralding in the stock market.

The conventional prudential surveillance frameworks are displaying a shortsightedness and are valid exclusively for the short run disrespectfully of the requirement of proceeding to early warning and long run forecasting for the sake of annihilating the likelihood of unexpected outbursts of financial distress.

This is mainly due to the fact that the features that render financial crises and bank runs very harmful is the fact that they hit unexpectedly without allowing for a time span for the regulator to react in a curative manner and should therefore be maneuvered in advance following a certain scrutinizing of risk dispersion and moments which are the skew and Kurtosis.

Therefore the adopted preventive approaches that help upgrade the short run prudential frameworks and the early warning approach are the best fit for mitigating the likelihood of outburst of financial meltdowns.

Based on the theoretical underpinnings according to which financial instability is a tradeoff between stock market excess volatility and credit market risk and eventually insurance market risk in another instance of analysis, it is shown that the systemic character of risk forbids containing risk exposure simultaneously to the credit and stock market sectors and hence leads few room to synchronized rsk mitigationthrough the entire financial system.

Besides this upgrading that should be operated on the credit sector prudential apparatus there should be stock market prudential surveillance enhanced by recourse to artificial intelligence and neural networks as thoroughly discussed in Part 1.

Thorough resilience from financial instability eventhough extremely improved as the book discusses shoud be up dated according to current monetary policy adopted by central banks and other salient factors such as regional improvements in prudential practices that are rather quantitative than qualitative.

This book hence has portrayed an attempt to cover the qualitative aspect of enhancing prudential practices as this apparatus not only has revealed the last resort option after the ineffectiveness of monetary policy to make economies cope with the 2008 sub prime crisis but also has proven its effectiveness in many economies during the last decade.

References

1- Adrian, T., & Rosenberg, J. (2008). Stock Returns and Volatility: Pricing the Short Run and Long Run Components of Market Risk. The Journal of Finance, 63, 2997-3030.

2- Baker, M., & Wurgler, J. (2007). Investor Sentiment in the Stock Market. Journal of Economic Perspectives, 21, 129-152.

3- Chalova, A., Gromova, E., & Voronkova, E. (2019). Integration of the Financial Market Sectors: Factors, Risks and Management Approach. International journal of Mechanical Engineering and Technology, 1243-1250.

4- Daxhammer, R. J., & Kappler, J. (2016). The Examination of a Profitability-Based Four Factor Model to Explain Stock Returns: Empirical Evidence from the German Stock Market. ESB Business School Reutlinger University.

5- Dimson, E., & Mussavian, M. (1998). A Brief History of Market Efficiency. European Financial Management, 4, 91-193.

6- Dodd, R. (2000). The Role of Derivatives in the East Asian Financial Crisis. SCEPA Working Paper Series 2000-19, Schwartz Center for Economic Policy Analysis (SCEPA) the New School.

7- Dodd, R. (2002). Consequences of Liberalizing Derivatives Markets. Financial Policy Forum Washington DC Derivatives Study Center.

8- Eugene Fama and Kenneth R French (1992). The Cross Section of Expected Stock Returns. The Journal of Finance, 47, 427-465.

9- Fender (2000). The Impact of Corporate Risk Management on Monetary Policy Transmission: Some Empirical Evidence. Working Paper N 95, BIS Bank of International Settlements.

10- Joseph, S. E. (1982). The Inefficiency of the Stock Market Equilibrium. The Review of Economic Studies, 49, 241-261.

11- Modigliani, F., & Miller, M. H. (1958). The Cost of Capital, Corporation

Finance and the Theory of Investment. The American Economic Review, 48, 261-297.

12- Oliner, S. D., & Rudebusch, G. D. (1996). Monetary Policy and Credit Conditions: Evidence from the Composition of External Finance: Comment. The American Economic Review, 86, 300-309.

13- Pilinkus, D. (2010). Macroeconomic Indicators and Their Impact on Stock Market Performance in the Short Run and Long Run: The Case of the Baltic States. Technological and Economic Development of Economy, 16, 291-304.

14- Sajjad, F., Noreen, V., & Zaman, K. (2013). Imapct of Derivatives on Financial Services Sector and Risk Management. Middle East Journal of Scientific Research, 18, 748-758.

15- Shreya, A., & Sangeetha, R. (2019). The Impact of Macroeconomic Determinants on the Performance of the Indian Stock Market. International Journal of Business and Man-Agement Invention, 8, 16-23.

16- Son, I. S., Oh, K. J., Kim, T. Y., Kim, C., & Do, J.-D. (2009). Stock Market Stability Index: An Intelligent Approach. Intelligent Data Analysis, 13, 983-993.

17- Abdali Seja (2013), Toward a conceptual framework for integrating entrprises performance and risk management, Journal of Management research ISSN 1941-899x 2013 vol1 N 04

18- Beasley, Chen Nunez and Wright (2006), Working hand in hand : Balanced scoreard and entreprise rsk management Annual conference topic : Strategic finance and Risk management

19- Gordon, Loeba and Tseng (2009), ntrprise risk management and firm performance : a contingency perspective, Journal of accounting and public policy Elsevier vol 28 p 301-327

20- Dell'Aricca G (2001) Asymmetric information and the structure of the banking industry, European economic review, V 45 pp 1957-1980

21- Podpiera, Jiri and Weil laurent (2008) Bad luck or bad management ? Emerging banking experience, Journal of financial stability, Elsevier vol 4(2) p 135-148

22- P A Samuelson (1939) Paul Samuelson's legacy, Annual review of economics Princeton university

23- J R Hicks (1950) A contribution to the theory of the trade cycle , Clarendon Press

24- Frei Cristoph (2017), Modeling credit risk and loan portfolio in the presence of autocorrelation UBS University of Alberta

25-Yue Yu and Pavel Loskot (2022), Polynomial distributions and transformations ZJU-UIUC Institute Haining China

26-Yuhong Sheng and Kai Yoo (2014), Some formulas of variance of uncertain random variables, Journal of uncertainty analysis and applications

27-Adrian T and Rosenberg J (2008), Stock returns and volatility: pricing the short run and long run components of market risk, The journal of Finance V 63

28-Agrawal Shreya, Sangeetha R, (2019), The impact of macroeconomic determinants on the performance of the Indian Stock Market, International Journal of Business and Management invention, Volume 8 Issue 3 Series V pp 16-23

29-Stiglitz E. Joseph (1982) The inefficiency of the Stock Market Equili-brium, Review of Economic Studies (1982) XLIX, pp 241-261 Princeton University

30-Alla Chalova, Elena Gromova and Elena Voronkova (2019), Integration of the financial market sectors: Factors, Risks and management approach, International journal of mechanical engineering and technology pp 1243-1250

31-Ray Ball (2000) What do we know about stock market efficiency? Ma-nagerial economics research letters at the university of Rochester USA

32-Tak Kuen Siu (2010) A Markov regime-switching marked point process for short rate analysis with credit risk Department of actuarial studies, Faculty of business and economics, Macquire University Sydney NSW 2190 australia International journal of Stockastic analysis Volume 2010 Article ID 870516

33- Kim Tae Yun, Do Kyong and Son suh (2009) Stock market stability index: An intelligent approach, Intelligent data analysis, DOI 10-3235 pp 983-993

34-Sajjad F, Noreen V and Zaman K (2013), Imapct of derivatives on financial services sector and risk management, Middle east journal of scientific research ISSN 1990-9233

35-Rolf J Daxhammer and Jonathan Kappler (2016), The examination of a profitabilitybased four factor model to explain stock returns: Empirical evidence from the German Stock market, ESB Business School Reutlinger University

36-Goerge Akerlof (1970), the market of lemons, the quarterly journal of economics vol 84 pp 488-500

37-Stiglitz J and Weiss A (1981) Credit rationing in markets with imperfect information, The american economic review V 71 pp 393-410

38-Dell'Aricca G (2001) Asymmetric information and the structure of the banking industry, European economic review, V 45 pp 1957-1980

39- Lynn Aylward and Rupert Thorne (1998) Countries' repayment performance vis-à-vis the IMF, IMF staff papers a quarterly journal of the IMF V 45

40-Mishkin FS (1998) The economics of money Banking and financial markets, Editor : Addison Wesley Boston

41-Dell'Arricia (1998) Assymetric information and the structure of the banking industry, IMF working paper International Monetary Fund WP/98/92

42-Agrawal Shreya, Sangeetha R, March (2019), The impact of macroeconomic determi-nants on the performance of the Indian Stock Market, International Journal of Business and Management invention, Volume 8 Issue 3 Series V pp 16-23

43-Baker M and Wungler J (2006), Investor sentiment and the cross-section of stock re-turns, The journal of finance volume 6 Issue 4 Pages 1645 to 1680

44-Ball Ray What do we know about stock market efficiency ? Managerial economics re-search center at the university of Rockester and the John M Olin foundation

45-Dimson Elroy, Mussavian Massoud, March (1998), A brief history of market efficiency, European financial management, Vol 4, N 01 pp 91-193

46-Fei Wu, Dayong Zhang and Zhiwei Zhang (2018) Systemic risks and spillovers in the stock market of China : a sectoral analysis, Research institute of economics and management Southern universtity of finance and economics China.

47-Fortin Michel, Khoury Nabil T (1988), Effectiveness of hedging interest rates risks and stock market risks with financial fultures, The journal of futures markets Vol 8 N 3 pp 319-334

48-Gurcharan Singh and Salony Kansal (2010), Impact of derivatives trading on stock market volatility during pre and post Fand O period : A case study of NSE, School of management studies Punjabi university Patiala Volue 1 No 1

49-Joseph Stiglitz (1982), the inefficiency of the stock market equilibrium, Review of economic studies XLIX, pp 241-261

50-Malcolm Baker and Jeffery Wurgler (2007), Investor sentiment in the stock market, Journal of economic perspectives, Volume 21, Number 2 pages 129-151.

51-Peter Haiss and Bernhard Sammer (2010), The impact of derivatives markets on financial integratuion risk and economic growth, Institute of international business Vienna University of economics and business presented at the Athenian policy fo-rum 10th biennial conference on regulatory responses to the financial crisis Frankfurt 28-31 july 2010

52-Roberto Casarin and Carmine Trecroci (2007), Business cycle and stock market vola-tilities are they related ?, CEREMADE and department of economics Paris Dauphine Septemner 2007

53-Sahel Benjamin, Vesala Jukka (1999), Financial stability analysis using aggregated data, European Central Bank BIS papar N 01

54-Stiglitz E. Joseph (1982) The inefficiency of the Stock Market Equilibrium, Review of Economic Studies (1982) XLIX, pp 241-261 Princeton University

55- Genc (2012) Empirical estimation of elasticities and their use, Department of Economics University of Otago New Zealand

56-Banks J, R Bundell and A Lewbel (1997) Quadratic engel curves and consumer demand, Review of Economics and Statistics 79, 527-539

57- Board of Governers of the Federal Reserve System (2023) The FEDERAL RESERVE BANK

58- Abdali Seja (2013), Toward a conceptual framework for integrating enterprises performance and risk management, Journal of Management research ISSN 1941-899x 2013 vol1 N 04

59- Beasley, Chen Nunez and Wright (2006), Working hand in hand : Balanced scorecard and enterprise rsk management Annual conference topic : Strategic finance and Risk management

60- Gordon, Loeba and Tseng (2009), Enterprise risk management and firm performance : a contingency perspective, Journal of accounting and public policy Elsevier vol 28 p 301-327

61- Sahajwala and Bergh (2000), Supervisory risk assessment and early warning systems, Basel committee on banking supervision working papers

62- Zhang Y et al (2020), The impact of artificial intelligence and blockchain on the accounting profession, Open journal of accounting Vol 12 N 3 July (2020) DOI: https://.org/10.1109/ACCESS.2020.3000505

63- Cilingtroglu, Artificial intelligence in the stock market : Quantitative Technical Analysis, Model weight optimization and Financial sentiment : Evaluation to predict stock prices, Intersect journal vol17 N4 (2023)

64- Joseph, S. E. (1982). The Inefficiency of the Stock Market Equilibrium. The Review of Economic Studies, 49, 241-261.

65- Pilinkus, D. (2010). Macroeconomic Indicators and Their Impact on Stock Market Performance in the Short Run and Long Run: The Case of the Baltic States. Technological and Economic Development of Economy, 16, 291-304.

66- Dell'Aricca G (2001) Asymmetric information and the structure of the banking industry, European economic review, V 45 pp 1957-1980

67- Franklin R Edwards (1988) Policies to curb Stock market volatility, Columbia University

Publisher: Eliva Press Global Ltd

Email: info@elivapress.com

www.ingramcontent.com/pod-product-compliance
Lightning Source LLC
LaVergne TN
LVHW022108200926
848481LV00003B/1107
* 9 7 8 9 9 9 9 3 3 7 9 5 3 *